First published in Great Britain in 2008 by Prion
an imprint of the
Carlton Publishing Group
20 Mortimer Street
London W1T 3JW

10 9 8 7 6 5 4 3 2 1

A catalogue record for this book is available from the British Library

ISBN 978-1-85375-683-2

Printed in Dubai

THE CRAP OLD DAYS

WHY ALL THAT OLD STUFF WAS ACTUALLY RUBBISH

Wayne Williams and Darren Allan

PRION

NUMBERS

12-inch Remixes
3D Movies
3-2-1

A

Action Man
The Adventure Game
Atari VCS
The A-Team
Athena

B

The Bangles
Batteries Not Included
The Benny Hill Show
Big Glasses
Big Perms
Black-face Soap
Mr Blobby
Bodies
British Beer
Bros
Brut
Bucks Fizz
Bullseye

C

C64 versus Speccy
Cabbage Patch Kids
CB Radio
Charley Says
The Chopper
Clackers
The Clangers
Colour-changing
  T-shirts
Corona
Crackerjack
Crowded House
The Crystal Maze

D

Deeley Boppers
Designer Stubble
Dirty Dancing
Doctor Who
"Do They Know It's
  Christmas?"
Dragon's Lair
Dr Seuss
Dungeons & Dragons
Duran Duran

E

Eldorado
Etch-a-Sketch
Evel Knievel Stunt
  Cycle

F

Fake Ice Cubes
Fantasy Island
Femidom
Fighting Fantasy
First Generation VCRs
Flares
Flight Deck
The Flying Pickets
Ford Capri
Frankie Goes to
  Hollywood
Free School Milk

G

The Generation Game
Gobstoppers
Gonks
Grease
Green Shield Stamps
Green Slime
The Grifter

H

Head Bags
He-Man
Hi-de-Hi!

I

The Incredible Hulk
I-Spy
Izal

J

Jubbly
Junior Chemistry Set

K

Kaliber
Ketchips
Kia-Ora
Kim Wilde
Kipper Tie
Knight Rider
The Krankies

L

Leg Warmers
Lightsaber
Liquorice Root
London to Brighton
  in Three-and-a-Half
  Minutes
Love Bites

CONTENTS

INTRODUCTION

Look around at the world today and what do you see? Maybe there's a child on a street corner, wearing a hoody and stuffing Cheestring-wrapped Turkey Twizzlers into his foul-mouthed gob. Turn on the TV and Jeremy Kyle's ugly furrowed mug might be staring back out at you (come back Kilroy, all is… well, maybe not). Go for an evening out on the town and you might see a young lady squatting on the pavement outside a nightclub, relieving herself copiously as a couple of shaven-headed lads fight over who was first in the taxi queue. Then there's gun and knife crime, being mugged for your iPod, happy slappings…

So it's not surprising that post-millennium, it has become more and more tempting to look back dreamily at the past, longing for those innocent and carefree days when you could leave your front door unlocked, the family still ate meals around the table, and a poof was a small cushioned square you put your feet up on. However, it's become quite clear that our love affair with bygone decades has reached absurd levels.

Sure, *Life on Mars* and *Ashes to Ashes* were great – mostly thanks to Gene Hunt's delightful drubbing of political correctness – but did we really need to see Vernon Kay resurrecting mouldy old game shows on our TV screens? Or John Rambo blundering back into the movies, mowing down bad guys when he really should've been sat at home with a nice cup of cocoa, filling out his application for a free bus pass. How about all those oft-repeated programmes that they love to air, such as the *100 Greatest TV Characters*, *50 Greatest One Hit Wonders* and the *Top 10 Best Soap Scouring Pads from 1976*. You know, the ones so ludicrous in their warm embrace of the past, they often feature youthful TV presenters recalling products or programmes that existed before they were actually born. ("Ahh, wasn't *The Sweeney* wicked… my dad told me all about it…")

Now is the time to take off the rose-tinted glasses and be poked in the eye with the truth. The truth that much of the past was awful. In this book, we'll look back in anger and recall some of the horrors that yesteryear held. Travesties such as:

Roland Rat: Made his bubonic ancestors look positively appealing.
Sodastream: It was fizzy, but it sure as hell wasn't Coke.
Puffball Skirts: Woman meets lampshade, but definitely not an electric look.
Cabbage Patch Kids: Ugly, creepy, scary and pointless. And ugly.
Bros: Why were they, were they made famous?
Spot the Ball: You had more chance of spotting Lord Lucan.

Within these pages there are some obvious disaster areas, but you may find your hackles rising when you spot an old favourite toy or TV programme singled out for criticism. Just take a deep breath and remember it for how it truly was. Your recollections are likely to be tinged with the all-pervading positivity that nostalgia tends to foster, and your mind has probably swept some of the more negative memories under the neural carpet.

Just because you grew up with something doesn't make it good. Much about the 1970s and 1980s was dire. Read on and you'll soon start to remember just how shit the past was. The truth is that if you discovered a TARDIS on your doorstep tomorrow, you'd be better off vandalising it than travelling back in time and being forced to sit through the raising of the *Mary Rose* again.

Footnote:

The dates quoted for popularity are rough approximations of when things were at the height of their influence. They may have been (and indeed in many cases were) around earlier and/or later than this. Any comments on inaccuracies in the estimations of peak popularity should be written on the back of a postcard and sent to the relevant ombudsman at the following address:

> The Department of Pedantry,
> 213a Pointless Drive,
> Tossington
> P1S S0F

In the 1980s, if you liked a song you went out and bought the single on 7-inch vinyl. If you loved it you went out and bought the 12-inch version instead. This was an exciting innovation in popular music. Just as the Reliant Robin was created due to a shortage of wheels – what other reason could there be? – so the 12-inch came about when a mix engineer ran out of 7-inch discs. In any other job you'd get fired for incompetence and rubbish stock control, but putting a single on album vinyl was heralded as a great breakthrough by the music business. Of course, the packaging industry had been sticking tiny products in huge boxes for years (for some reason, Peter Andre and Jordan sprang to mind while writing that sentence).

The larger disc reproduced the audio better, or so we were told, due to the extra groove space. Not that you could tell. You'd probably be able to find more men who could correctly identify the difference between Bright White, Pure White and Snow White paints than people who were perceptive enough to pick up the variance in audio quality. Listeners who claimed they could hear the improvement were either liars, or worked for HMV (and were lying).

Of course, slapping the same song on a larger disc and charging more money for it was never going to fool everyone, so the record companies came up with a plan – the 12-inch remix. The theory was simple. If you liked a song a whole lot, you'd want to hear more of it. So they took the track and added to it, making it longer to fill up space. These extended versions were generally referred to as dance remixes on account of the fact they sure as hell weren't listening remixes.

The phrase "too much of a good thing" was clearly not something that record producers understood, because 12-inch mixes typically went on forever. You'd put a track on, listen to it for five minutes, check the label to make sure it was the song you thought you'd bought, go into town with your mates, shoplift some pick 'n' mix from Woollies, buy *Smash Hits,* 15 cans of hairspray and a Rubik's cube, go home, read your mag, style your hair, solve the puzzle and return to your bedroom just in time to catch the bit of the song you actually recognized and liked – the 7-inch section. Once that finished you could go out, safe in the knowledge that you still had hours to go until the finale (five electronic handclaps and a fadeout).

After ten years of remixes, the CD arrived and the 12-inch single became a thing of the past. Record companies haven't produced them in years (not in any great quantity, anyway) and yet despite this there are still tracks playing which are only now, after all this time, finally getting to the good bit.

Stereoscopic films have been around since the 1920s, but the 1950s was unquestionably the medium's golden age, with excited teenagers flocking to the cinema to see such classics as *The House Of Wax, Dial M for Murder* and *The French Line* (or "Jane Russell in 3D!" as it was marketed). The format fell out of favour in the 1960s, replaced by drugs which, if taken in the right quantities, could make everything come at you in freaky 3D. Even things which only existed inside your mind.

3D movies made a short-lived return in the 1980s, possibly because so much time had elapsed that people had forgotten how shit they actually were. You didn't have to spend very long watching one to quickly be reminded.

The thing with 3D films is the plot doesn't actually matter. It's not about whether boy meets girl, girl meets boy, they fall in love and then he dies at the hands of a sadistic Nazi captain; it's about a man with a stick. There doesn't even need to be an especially good reason why he's got that stick. All that has to happen is at some point in the film, he's required to poke it out towards the camera, so in 3D terms it looks as if it's coming right out at the audience. A load of bees buzzing around the auditorium, a man with a flyswatter, and probably a ladder that gets swung out and/or falls over are also all guaranteed to make an appearance at some stage.

The other downside of 3D films is they really aren't date movies. For starters, to see them – in 3D at least – you're required to wear stupid glasses. Probably with red and green lenses. These make you look a prat. Your date looks like a prat too, but not as much as you do. If you wear specs, then you look twice the prat. That in itself is bad enough, but the biggest problem comes later. Prolonged exposure to a 3D film means that you're guaranteed to have a headache afterwards, so sex is certainly off the menu.

What really stalled the 3D movie revival in the 1980s was the choice of films available though. *Jaws 3D* was possibly the worst offender, although *Amityville 3D, Friday the 13th Part 3* and *Freddy's Dead: The Final Nightmare (*aka *A Nightmare on Elm Street 6)* all took turns to hammer nails into the medium's coffin.

Despite this, like Freddy Krueger and Jason Voorhees, 3D movies just refuse to die. Thankfully, these days they are mainly confined to kids' films which means you can put the glasses on, get comfy and then go to sleep when the movie starts. So long as you realize you're likely to be woken up part way through by an audience of children all demanding to know the same thing. "Why's that man got a stick?"

9

Ted Rogers was the host of this popular 1980s game show. He must have spent days, maybe weeks or even months solidly rehearsing for the role when he first landed it. Not because the show was executed perfectly or anything – just to learn how to do the famous *3–2–1* gesture. This involved him putting three fingers up, then swiftly changing it to two then one as he swivelled his hand dexterously about like some sort of palm magician.

The programme was called *3–2–1* because it was divided into three rounds, the first of which was a simple quiz. The second was an elimination round. Sadly it didn't involve shooting all the contestants with bad perms and dodgy mullets, but instead featured some basic game – the computer game Breakout in the later shows. All this was easy enough up until the last round, when the straightforward suddenly transformed into the inconceivably fiendish.

In this round the finalists were tortured twice over, once by a series of variety acts who would come on and perform, and secondly by the clues these acts gave them. Each clue consisted of an object and a rhyme which represented a prize, from a car or a holiday through to the booby prize, Dusty Bin – a plastic robot dustbin (you didn't actually win Dusty, just a shiny new bin, although that was probably worth more anyway).

Eventually, the last couple playing ended up with a number of clues on the table and they had to work out which prizes these might correspond to, getting rid of the crap ones and hopefully ending up with a winner. For example, there might be a key as an object and a rhyme containing the word "garage." The contestants would keep this, thinking that "garage" indicated a car, with the key serving as a car key. Then Ted would explain what it actually was, which would go something like this:

3-2-1's infamous booby prize – that tit Ted Rogers.

"What do you associate a key with? Well, it opens something, usually a door. Now the rhyme mentioned a garage and of course a garage has a door, but what's it made out of? Usually some sort of light metal, perhaps tin. And what's made out of tin, and what rhymes with tin? Yes, it's bin, and here's old Dusty, I'm so sorry folks…"

The clues were just so stupidly obtuse that solving them was impossible – you had more chance of successfully emulating Ted's trademark *3–2–1* motion. And I bet many contestants tried the latter, or a modified interpretation using only two and one fingered gestures, after they'd heard the utter bullshit solution.

Action Man — Toy popular around 1970–84

Action Man was the action figure with more accessories than Vivienne Westwood. He had different outfits you could put on, little plastic boots, belts, scarves, false wartime papers… all sorts of useless crap. Red Devil Action Man even had his own parachute, so you could fling him out of your bedroom window. The 'chute never actually unfolded properly – what with it essentially being an orange carrier bag – so he inevitably hit the pavement at speed, with a plastic limb-shattering thump.

Luckily, he had about a hundred different modes of transport to reach the nearest field hospital, including the fondly remembered tank (complete with turret and driver hatches), armoured car, jeep, horse, dinghy and Sinclair C5. Okay, so he never drove a C5 – he might have been stupid enough to jump out of a second storey window attached to a brightly painted Sainsbury's bag, but he didn't have a complete death-wish.

If you wanted a more intelligent Action Man, you could always buy the articulate officer known as the Talking Commander. You pulled the cord attached to his back and he uttered various military phrases such as "Action Man patrol, fall in!", "Enemy aircraft! Action stations!",

Even today, mass Action Men graves are still uncovered in gardens throughout Britain.

"Volunteer needed for a special mission" and "Don't throw me out of the bedroom window you little bastaaaaaggghhh!" If you did throw him out of the window, or took him for a swim, you soon found the Talking Commander had a lot less to say for himself.

Aside from the plethora of money-spinning extras Palitoy flogged alongside him, the traditional Action Man was famous for his bristly fake hair and the range of "thrilling" actions he could perform. He had dynamic movable limbs, and gripping hands that could hold a gun. Not to mention eagle eyes that could look around. I suspect that all this was scant consolation for having no penis, but there you go.

Despite his plastic moulded pants with no contents, and the fact that action was the one thing he was certainly never going to get, he was still popular with the girls. Well my sister at least. She stole my Action Man to be her Barbie's boyfriend because Ken was such a fucking soppy drip, and the army bloke had more of a macho edge. It was that cool scar on his face that did it. Admittedly he had less of an edge when I finally found him in Barbie's summer villa having afternoon tea, dressed in a tuxedo and now apparently called Paul. Only a girl would actually name an Action Man.

Like all army deserters, Paul had to be taken out and shot, in the back garden, with an air rifle. No matter how much my sister cried.

The Adventure Game — TV Programme popular around 1980–86

These days it's generally only rednecks living in America's Deep South who get abducted by aliens. In the early 1980s – if you believe *The Adventure Game* at least – extraterrestrials spent most of their time chumming around with crap British TV celebrities. Famous names like Keith Chegwin, Bonnie Langford, Nerys Hughes, Derek Griffiths and Duncan Goodhew all chose to boldly go where no man had gone before. These stars weren't actually abducted, but rather they made their own way across the universe, eventually arriving on an alien world called Arg. This was described as being "a planet of little consequence", making it the perfect place for celebrities of zero consequence to land.

Because bad things always happen in threes, there were always three celebs in each visiting party – someone clever, someone off kids' TV, and someone you'd never heard of. Unfortunately for them, the inhabitants of the planet, a race of shape-shifting fluffy lizard things called Argonds, felt that the right and proper way of welcoming galactic neighbours was to set them various logic puzzles and cryptic challenges to overcome, and televise the results. (This was preferable to the alternative though, which was to lock them up for ten weeks in the Argond Brother house).

The tests and challenges were designed, apparently, to gauge the wit and perspicacity of the visitors, although faced with the likes of Cheggers I'd have thought testing for intelligence with the traditional anal probe might have been more appropriate. After assessing 22 groups of thick-as-pig-shit celebrities, it's no surprise that aliens now prefer to run their experiments on slack-jawed southern inbreeds called Bubba. At least there's a chance of finding some trace of sentience there.

The Argonds were an unquestionably odd race. For starters, all their names were anagrams of the word Dragon. There was Rangdo, the planet's ruler, Gandor, Gnoard, Dorgan, Darong and Rongad. R. Gonad never put in an appearance, sadly, which was surprising given the amount of dicks on the show.

Gandor was an ancient, half-deaf butler, Dorgan was a patronising simpleton and Rongad spoke backwards with an Australian accent. He would praise contestants by saying "doog yrev" which meant very good. It was an annoying trait and it's no wonder that behind his back Rongad was referred to as that "reknaw gnikcuf."

The Argonds each had distinct human forms, which they changed into before the contestants arrived. This was ostensibly to avoid scaring the guests with their true appearance. However, seeing that their true forms looked as if they'd just stepped off the set of a particularly low-budget episode of *Doctor Who*, the shape change was probably necessary to prevent the contestants pissing themselves with laughter. At any rate, if they wanted to avoid scaring visitors they really should have banned Darong from transforming into newsreader Moira Stuart

Rangdo clearly didn't fancy being either a dragon or a human, so spent much of his time disguised as an irritably-burbling aspidistra or, in the final series, a teapot. He still demanded respect however, and all visitors had to bow or curtsey and placate him with the phrase "gronda, gronda," which turned out to be another meaningless dragon anagram they had left over.

The challenges facing the contestants varied from show to show, but you could guarantee they would include a stepping stone puzzle based around drogna (Arg's colourful – and anagrammed – currency), and some crappy maze game played on a BBC Acorn computer.

When they'd managed to complete all of the tasks, the team would face one final challenge – the Vortex. This involved walking across a grid-like gantry that bridged a chasm with the universe stretching to infinity below. Taking it one move at a time, contestants had to step from point to point (forwards, backwards or sideways) with the aim being to make it to the end and successfully avoid the Vortex, an embarrassingly amateurish computer graphic which also moved one spot at a time. We could see this superimposed squiggle, but the contestants couldn't – which was where the fun lay.

Watching Keith Chegwin step on to the section occupied by the Vortex and get evaporated was the main reason to tune in. Or rather the only reason. When the contestants somehow avoided the Vortex – usually thanks to the ham sandwich – we all felt seriously cheated.

Atari VCS   Games Console popular around 1977–90

VCS most definitely didn't stand for Very Crap System. Although it should have.

In 1977, Atari brought the arcade into the home with its Video Computer System, later renamed as the Atari 2600. This was a major breakthrough in home entertainment. There had been games consoles before, but this was the first to offer a choice of games – not just Pong. With the VCS we could experience the joys of cutting-edge arcade classics like Space Invaders, Frogger and Pac-Man on our living room televisions. Provided *Some Mothers Do 'Ave 'Em* or *Coronation Street* wasn't on at the same time, naturally.

You plugged in the games cartridge, switched on the console and prepared to be amazed. The graphics were incredible. We stared at them open-mouthed in disbelief, unable to comprehend what we were seeing. What, we all wanted to know, was this shit supposed to be? VCS games basically involved a bunch of crap coloured blocks flickering slowly across the screen, accompanied by a bleeping racket. They had about as much in common with their arcade counterparts as instant noodles had with food. Still, there was always the game play to enjoy. Or there would have been if that wasn't equally limp. In truth, the only good thing about the console was the fact that it didn't look out of place in the living room, what with its fetching woodgrain appearance perfectly complementing the decor in most 1970s homes.

Despite being about as technically advanced as the Ronco Buttoneer, the Atari VCS, with its plastic paddles and stubby joysticks, went on to sell around 40,000,000 consoles to disappointed idiots around the world. The company was still successfully flogging them at the start of the 1990s, even though we should have all known better by then. Mind you, it was a revised and improved version at that point... Atari had swapped the woodgrain casing for a black plastic one. Which just goes to show, if you can't polish a turd, paint it.

The A-Team — TV Programme popular around 1983–87

The A-Team was great wasn't it? The ultimate 1980s TV show – well, that and *Miami Vice*. Hey, do you remember that episode where the pretty girl with the big hair went looking to hire the A-Team but couldn't find them? And just when she was about to give up, Hannibal revealed himself (in a non-sexual way) as having been there the whole time but in disguise? Hilarious!

Then they had to bust Murdoch out of the psychiatric hospital where he was staying, before roaring off to a deserted airfield in their distinctive black van. But when they got there BA said – I love this scene – "I ain't getting on no plane!" and they had to drug his milk and then drag him on-board.

Don't you just love it when a photo comes together?

And, you'll remember this part as well, how when trying to solve the girl's problems they got into a gunfight and shot that car out, which careered over the edge of a cliff, somersaulting through the air and landing on its roof. Thankfully no one inside was hurt. Then the A-Team managed to get away and hole up in that shed, which luckily was owned by a welder who'd left six oxyacetylene gas tanks lying around. They used those to build a kooky tank out of old car exhausts, planks of wood and cabbages, which was employed to finally overcome the bad guys. Face got to snog the girl at the end. It was a classic episode wasn't it? You remember it, surely?

You should do. It was the same bastard show every single week. The sole variation was the disguises that Hannibal wore, which ranged from the improbable lizard suit, to the downright dodgy 'blacked-up with an afro' look. It's surprising BA didn't punch his lights out in that episode.

Other than that, the show was a running template. Hannibal loved it when a plan came together, and BA thought that Murdoch was a crazy fool who required pitying, which was generally true. But not as crazy or foolish as the audience who tuned in every week to a new episode which was exactly the sodding same as the one the week before.

Athena
Poster Shop popular around 1980–96

Posters were massive in the 1970s and 1980s. In terms of size as well as sales. Everyone had at least one up on their bedroom wall and it was generally large enough to hide a secret tunnel behind. When you wanted to buy a new poster, there was only one place to go: Athena. It stocked every poster ever printed, although it mostly only sold four designs – the tennis girl scratching her bum, the male model with the baby, dolphins leaping over a setting sun, and Ché Guevara.

In the mid-1990s, when people decided smaller posters or framed prints were the way to go, Athena ran into problems and eventually went bankrupt. The potentially company-saving image – a shirtless Ché Guevara clawing his hairy arse while cradling a toddler in his dolphin-tattooed arm – sadly never made it into production.

The Bangles
Pop Group popular around 1986–88

They might have walked like Egyptians, but they sounded like a load of starving cats entombed in a pyramid.

Batteries Not Included   Box Comment popular around 1960–90

Why the fuck not? You charge enough for the toy. Would it really hurt your profits to sling in a couple of AA batteries to avoid disappointment on Christmas day? Cheap bastards.

The Benny Hill Show   TV Programme popular around 1969–89

Comedy has a number of laws. For example, it's a well known fact that lists of funny things always come in threes. You can never have two funny things, or four. It's invariably three. Another rule of comedy is that someone called Benny is usually highly amusing. Benny from *Crossroads* – he was hilarious! Benny Andersson from ABBA had one of the most comical beards ever. The myopic antics of Benny from *Top Cat* (or *Boss Cat* as it used to be known) were always good for a laugh... And then there's Benny Hill. As I was saying, funny things always come in threes.

Benny played the toy-maker in Chitty Chitty Bang Bang.
And the twat in The Benny Hill Show.

17

Inside you there's this wacky, zany and crazy half-mad character just bursting to get out, but the problem is poor eyesight and an aversion to contact lenses means you're forced to wear glasses. And they, unfortunately, give you an air of unwanted and studious respectability. Not to worry though – the answer is right in front of your half-blind eyes. All you have to do to unleash your madcap personality is super-size those spectacles!

In the 1980s, all it took to appear mental was a pair of huge specs. Or outrageous specs. Or better yet, huge outrageous specs. Elton John had been doing it for a while, as had Dame Edna Everage, but in the mid-1980s the fashion really took hold. You couldn't turn on the telly without being confronted by a glasses-wearer sporting jumbo frames. There was Timmy Mallett, Mark Curry, Christopher Biggins, Ken Morley, Su Pollard, DJ Mike Read, weatherman Ian McCaskill and snooker player Dennis Taylor… all wearing extra-large bins, and the public loved them. Especially Taylor, who was so blind he didn't even know he was wearing his glasses upside down! How mad is that? Eventually the fad died out, and people started wearing normal specs again. These days large frames have suddenly and inexplicably made a minor comeback, but this time thanks to another breed of crazy person – the footballer's wife.

How you doin'?

Big Perms

Short for "permanent wave", the perm was a chemical treatment which curled your hair. And everyone else's when they saw what you'd done to yourself.

It wasn't only women who took pride in looking like stupidly oversized shaggy poodles. Unbelievably, some men did too. Top footballers like Kevin Keegan started the trend back in the 1970s when they sported the likes of the bubble perm – although maybe that was just to distract everyone from those ridiculously tight footy shorts the players wore at the time.

When the 1980s arrived, the perm really made it big. The bigger the perm, the better, no matter how much of an arse it made you look. Some perms were so vastly bouffant, the bushy monstrosities needed a gardener to trim them, never mind a hairdresser. It was wise to take a pair of topiary shears with you to the cinema, in case you ended up sat behind someone with a big perm, so you could prune out a reasonably sized viewing area from the top of their heads (and maybe make it look like a swan at the same time).

Thankfully, as the decade drew to a close, people began to come to their senses, and if you persisted in having a power-perm hairdo it probably wasn't the only permanent wave you'd be getting; you could add a permanent goodbye wave from your long-suffering partner as well.

Welcome to the 1980s – the bad hair decade.

Black-face Soap | Practical Joke popular around 1955–85

This was a bar of soap, hollowed out and filled with some powdered nigrosine dye. The hole was covered with a paper label which wasn't waterproof. The idea was an unsuspecting person would splash water on their face, rub the soap with their hands, soaking the label and releasing the dye as they did so. This dye would mix with the soapy lather to make a black mess which they'd rub all over their face, while you guffawed through the crack in the bathroom door.

However, this idea was blatantly never going to work in a million years. Often the label didn't come off, or if it did the person saw the dye before it came out. If they did get it on their hands, they just rinsed it off. The only ones who might possibly have washed their faces in a dark grey lather and not noticed were blind people and the acutely stupid, and you could probably have got them to shower with a bottle of ink if you tried. Interestingly – or not – there's no evidence the black community ever bothered to produce white-faced soap.

Mr Blobby | Character popular around 1991–97

Jesus. Was there ever a bigger twat on Saturday night television? That bearded git Edmonds ensured *Noel's House Party* was truly painful viewing. And Mr Blobby didn't help either.

Blobby was a giant pink plastic creature covered in yellow spots who was first introduced on the "Gotcha" segment of the show, where

Two good reasons not to watch television in the 1990s.

celebrities were set up in Jeremy Beadle-style pranks. They would be trying to make a serious film of something or other and Blobby would blunder about, falling over and knocking down the set while constantly shouting "Blobby-blobby-blobby-blob-blob-blobby!" in a strange synthesized electronic voice.

And okay, this was vaguely amusing slapstick the first couple of times you saw it, particularly the Will Carling Gotcha in which the rugby player almost ended up punching Blobby's lights out. But the repetition of the same joke over and over and over wore thin quicker than a bar of soap in a nun's bath.

Yet for some unfathomable reason Blobby's popularity sky-rocketed and he popped up all over the place on various TV shows. The character also flogged loads of merchandise such as Blobby dolls, and even had a Christmas number one single in 1993. Still, at least it wasn't Cliff.

Inevitably Blobby's star faded, and as the 1990s were ushered out, so was the moronic pink nincompoop. Like many fallen celebs, rumour has it he squandered his fortune and is now out on the streets charging 50 pence a go – as a bouncy castle on the Golden Mile in Blackpool.

Bodies
Clothes popular around 1989–92

When you tuck in a shirt, eventually it's likely to come untucked. So you tuck it in again. Not really much of a problem. But clearly in the late 1980s it was a major concern for women, because they went out and bought bodies. Not from Burke and Hare, but more likely from Top Shop. Bodies were essentially fancy leotards that women wore away from the gym. They were skin-tight undergarments worn as overgarments and fastened at the crotch with poppers.

They stopped the untucked look, but when a woman wore one she was guaranteed to go unfucked too, as they were pretty much the modern day equivalent of the chastity belt. As if bras weren't complicated enough, here was another set of obstacles for the impatient man to try and overcome before getting down to business. Assuming a date got that far of course, and he didn't get bored and go home while waiting for the girl to do herself up in the toilets.

British Beer
Drink popular around 1960–79

It may seem difficult to believe now, but there was a time when Britain's favourite beer wasn't lager. And when it didn't come from Germany, Australia or Denmark, but was actually made in this country. Mind you, British beer certainly wasn't anything to be proud of. There's a good reason we were more than happy to abandon it when something more palatable finally arrived on these shores. And it's the same reason we no longer drool over the thought of pig's feet in jelly, or bread and dripping.

The most famous British brewer was Watney's, who gave us Red Barrel, a fizzy bitter on tap – later just called Watney's Red, as in "better dead than Red" – and the Party Four and Party Seven take-home varieties which contained (nearly) four and seven pints respectively. That may not sound like much of a party, but each was a barrel of fun. Especially when it came to opening it. If you didn't allow the can to settle for a while beforehand the beer would spray everywhere, generally soaking the unfortunate idiot trying to get into it and anyone stupid enough to be standing nearby offering advice. Naturally, those who experienced this impromptu golden shower would be left hopping mad and, no doubt, barley able to contain their rage.

Another popular beer was Double Diamond, a pale ale mostly remembered for its adverts which claimed it "worked wonders" to the tune of "There's a Hole in my Bucket". Exactly how it worked wonders was never revealed. Worked wonders at getting you rat-arsed possibly, or making your sister's ugly friend look gorgeous? Or maybe the slogan referred to the adverts themselves, which worked wonders at getting people to buy what was, essentially, a stumpy can of tasteless piss.

A giant's can of beer.
Yours for only three magic beans.

Bros

There were three members of Bros – Matt, Luke and Craig. Matt and Luke were blonde twins, while Craig looked nothing like either of them and had brown hair. Which suggests that he was either the result of an affair, or he'd been adopted. Although his completely different surname rather gave away the fact that they weren't actually all brothers. What a bloody swizz.

The group were mostly famous for their haircuts (which were shaved at the sides and back, and longish and slicked back on top) and their fashion style which involved ripped jeans and Grolsch bottle tops stuck on their shoes. Now I may be wrong, but I'm thinking that's a look which isn't ever likely to come back into fashion.

Matt sang, Luke drummed and Craig played the guitar. Matt actually had quite a reasonable voice, but it was spoilt by some odd vocal ticks. Every so often, in mid-sentence he'd growl his words like a wounded dog, do a whoop, or suddenly and inexplicably shout "Oo-er!" as if he suffered from the lesser-known Frankie Howerd strain of Tourettes. The band's first hit was "When Will I Be Famous?" The obvious answer should have been never. This song was followed up with "Drop the Boy", then "I Owe You Nothing", which – oo-er! – proved to be correct, because I wasn't stupid enough to buy a copy of the record. If I had done, they would've owed me at least a 99 pence refund because it was easily one of the most atrocious songs of the 1980s. And this – oo-er! – was around the same time Jason Donovan was recording, so they were besting some particularly dire competition.

Eventually Craig left the band and the twins limped on for a while longer, before finally giving up. At which point, it has to be said, I did owe them something. A round of applause and a massive thank you for finally shutting up. Oo-er!

Brut

Back in the days before aftershaves became sophisticated (and somewhat poncey) fragrances, men were limited to a handful of choices. They all came with suitably macho names: Denim, Hai Karate, Old Spice, Chaz and the king of them all, Brut. The name might have been spelt differently, but there was no mistaking the meaning. This was a fragrance for real men. I'm surprised they didn't go a step further and call it Thug or Bastard.

To reinforce its macho mystique, Brut was advertised by sportsmen like Henry Cooper and Kevin Keegan, who advised a gullible buying public to "splash it all over." Faberge got to sell loads more bottles on the back of the slogan – people "splashed it all over" and therefore ran out much quicker than if they'd "dabbed it on sparingly" – but it did mean that men everywhere stank to high heaven. "The great smell of Brut" it was referred to. "The great stench" would have been more appropriate.

There were actually two versions of the aftershave – Brut and Brut 33. Brut 33 was a lighter variety. Or to be more precise it was a cheaper, watered down concoction with 33% fragrance and 67% water. It was still overpowering though. If you wore Brut, you were guaranteed to take away the breath of any passing lady. Literally. And strip the paint from the wall she had collapsed against, too.

Bucks Fizz — Pop Group popular around 1981–86

This four-piece group achieved fame by winning *Eurovision* for Britain in 1981. The highlight of their on-stage routine came when the two guys raunchily ripped off the two girl's skirts… revealing not, as you might expect these days, pubic hair shaved into the shape of the Union Flag, but simply two more skirts. Scandalous. After their Euro triumph, they returned to these shores and sold loads of sickly sweet pop singles. Now that really was outrageous. But were they bloody rubbish or simply shit? To be honest I'm still making my mind up.

Bullseye — TV Programme popular around 1981–95

Darts was a ridiculously popular sport in the 1980s, but that doesn't really explain why someone designed a game show around it. Mullets were popular too, but they didn't get turned into a Sunday afternoon quiz show now did they? ("Long at the back, short on top – let's play Mullet!")

Instead we got *Bullseye*. The show was hosted by Jim Bowen, a man who referred to everything as "super", "smashing" or "great", even if it was boring, stupid or shit. He had support from his sidekick Tony 'take yer time' Green and Bully, the show's cartoon mascot, whose entire purpose was to slide in from the edge of the screen and snort. Presumably with derision at the audience for watching this load of twaddle.

The game began with three pairs of contestants. Each team had someone to throw darts and someone to answer questions based on the result of the throw. There were various rounds with different boards, just to make it nearly interesting. Personally I think the darts player being allowed to lob a dart at his team-mate if he got the answer wrong would have made matters more entertaining.

As the show progressed, two teams got knocked out, and the remaining pair progressed to Bully's Prize Board, where the key was to hit the narrow red segments and win prizes – mostly crap ones like some plates, a vase, or a Goblin Teasmade, which isn't half as much fun to wake up to as it sounds. If they hit the bull, they landed Bully's Special Prize (a set of encyclopaedias). The tension was unbearable. Like watching dried paint remain dry.

Once the round was over the contestants had a chance to gamble what they'd already won for a crack at the top prize. You had to score 101 or more with six darts to secure it, but the problem was the non-darts player had to throw three of them, so the teams rarely succeeded. Especially when Aunty Ethel had been brought along to answer the questions, and had to chuck her arrows while steadying herself with one hand on her zimmer-frame.

After the finalists had fluffed it, Bowen would trot out his favourite catchphrase – "Look at what you could have won" – and the producers would torture the contestants by wheeling out one of the more spectacular prizes, like a car or four-berth caravan.

On the rare occasions the players did win they always seemed to miss out on the automobile, ending up with something more budget friendly instead, like a suite of white goods. Or if they were really unlucky they might get to take home the infamous speedboat. The further away from the coast the winning contestants lived, the more likelihood there was of it appearing as the star prize. No doubt the duck ponds around Birmingham were filled with the buggers.

Regardless of whether they won or not, every contestant left with a set of darts, a tankard, a rubber Bendy Bully and a pat on the back from Jim. Though it probably felt like a pat on the back from Bully, given the inescapable feeling that they'd just been shat on.

C64 versus Speccy   Debate popular around 1983–86

In the early 1980s a Cold War was raging. You can forget the nonsense between America and the USSR, this was much more serious than that. This was a real war and you had to choose your side, and choose carefully. To join up all you had to do was know – beyond a shadow of a doubt – the answer to one simple question, and it was this: "Which is the best home computer on the planet?"

The answers were a) Commodore 64 or b) ZX Spectrum. If you were foolish enough to answer c) BBC Micro or worse still d) Dragon 32, then you could expect to be treated as some kind of social outcast. Going to school in a pink leotard three sizes too small with a large hole around the crotch would have been less embarrassing than admitting you owned an Oric or a Jupiter Ace.

The C64 was clearly the best home computer because it was the most powerful. It had 64k of memory, not 16k or 48k like the Spectrum. But, no, actually the Speccy was the better computer because it had the greatest games. Yeah, but the C64 had a real keyboard. So what? The Speccy had rubber keys which were better for playing its vastly superior games with. The argument went on and on, and there could never be a true winner because it was such an emotive subject.

Time has passed, however, and the home computer Cold War has thawed enough for me to finally end the great debate once and for all. To give you the definitive answer. So which was the best home computer on the planet, the Commodore 64 or the ZX Spectrum? Neither. They were both utter shit. Get over it.

The mighty Speccy. There were Magimix blenders with more processing power.

Cabbage Patch Kids   Toy popular around 1982–88

The Cabbage Patch Kids were sold off the back of their, ahem, charm. Each doll was an individual, sporting a unique hairstyle, clothes and facial features such as dimples. It even came with its very own name freshly inked onto an adoption certificate.

It was hardly surprising they were put up for adoption in the first place though. Any right-minded parent who'd seen one of these grotesquely ugly little bastards pop out onto the delivery table would be down the orphanage with a basket before the blood had dried. Or indeed, before the mud had dried in this case, as the loathsome looking sods were born – so the legend of the toy went – in a cabbage patch.

If they did come from a vegetable garden, it was one sprayed with massive doses of potent pesticides, judging by the doll's repulsively malformed faces. There's no denying they certainly looked like they'd been dug up from the ground, or more to the point, been beaten about the head with a shovel.

Yet despite their abominable aesthetics, they sold over 50,000,000 in the 1980s. And the creator of the dolls, Xavier Roberts, signed every single one on the left arse cheek. That must have given him one hellish bout of repetitive-strain-injury.

Of course, he never signed each Cabbage Patch Kid by hand any more than, as the back of the box claimed, he discovered the dolls in an "enchanted cabbage patch." Clearly they were made in a less-than-enchanted Asian factory, and a machine stamped the signatures on their butts. After all, only a powerful computer could reliably and consistently tell the difference between their arses and faces. Did I mention they were ugly?

Never mind Xavier's scribble, they should've made the final machine on the production line put a paper bag over each doll's head. They'd have sold even more then, as sane people and those with 20/20 vision might have been duped into buying one.

The Kids were scarier than a midnight clown convention.   **27**

The idea of Citizens' Band radio was that it allowed people – well, lorry drivers mainly – to chat with each other while travelling. If your vehicle was equipped with a CB set, you could alert fellow road users to motoring hazards such as speed traps, traffic jams, accidents or, most perilously of all, really expensive Little Chefs.

Chatting about traffic conditions might not seem particularly exciting, but CB was seen as thrilling stuff because it came with its very own language. You could only successfully talk to someone on the radio if you knew the proper lingo. A typical CB conversation went something like this:

"Breaker, breaker, one-niner this is Moonshine, got your ears on? Some flip-flopping bears just dusted my britches so you'd best put your flaps down. I'm going like a raped ape, got one foot on the floor, one hanging out the door, and she just won't do no more! Seventy-thirds good buddy."

Which, roughly translated means: "Hello, I'm a fucking idiot who watches lots of American movies and dreams of being Burt Reynolds. I've even grown a moustache like his. Would you like to stroke it?"

Everyone on CB had to have a 'handle'. Not a broom handle round the back of the head, sadly, but a nickname. The stupider and more outrageous the better. If you were going to be taken seriously on the radio you needed a cool name like Fluff, Cuddly Ken, The Hairy Cornflake or Simon Bates. And the same was true on CB.

Despite it being illegal to use an unlicensed radio transmitter in the UK, the CB craze spread like wildfire, thanks mainly to the appeal of movies such as *Convoy*, *Smokey and the Bandit* and *Breaker! Breaker*! Everyone knew someone who had a CB set and you could easily spot other users. The giveaway was the generally massive antennae, which looked fine on a ten tonne rig, bloody stupid on a Ford Granada, and just fantastic on a Sinclair C5, where it helped to enhance that "straight from the dodgems" look. Some people even installed CB radios in their houses – homebases – which was missing much of the point of it. You weren't likely to outrun Smokey (the police) in your Wimpey home, and knowing where the traffic jams were was of little use to listeners sat hunched over the kitchen table in their Y-fronts. Today's equivalent of a homebase would be trying to spark up an email conversation with a stranger by offering them your postal address. "Yes, it's Geoff@27WindsorGardensLowestoftSuffolkNR32ZB. Dot-com."

CB radio became so popular that in 1981 the government was forced to legalize it, which had the effect of instantly diminishing its appeal. After that it was downhill all the way, and a matter of years later CB had pretty much pulled the big one, ten-four, rubber duck. Which loosely means, well I'm not quite sure, but I think it's got something to do with having a wank in the bath.

Charley Says — Public Information Films popular around 1970–80

Charley was a ginger cartoon cat (voiced by Kenny Everett) who starred in a series of public information films throughout the 1970s. He was the pet of a small child, who in the short video clips would be about to do something dangerous, like play with matches, talk to strangers or mess about on a riverbank. Charley would then warn the boy against what he was going to get involved in. Or so we were led to believe. What Charley actually said was something like: "Meeeoowwww-rraaoow-rrrahhh-grreowww-raoww-grraghh-meowww-yeoooow."

The boy, who evidently spoke cat, would then translate for us. Of course, we've only got the little lad's word for it that these feline outpourings were indeed safety slogans born of concern for its owner. What with cats generally being self-centred creatures, Charley's much more likely to have actually said something like: "Oooh, I think I've got a fur ball in my throat. Ack, ack. Definitely something there. Put those matches down boy, and give me the Heimlich Manoeuvre before I choke."

"Is it time for food? It's got to be time for food? Stop pissing around with that man we've never seen before and feed me."

"Why are we outside mucking about near this river? Let's go inside and sit by the fire. I've been awake for nearly five minutes now. I'm getting dizzy with exhaustion."

The Chopper — Bicycle popular around 1975–80

Kids, eh? You gotta love them, but you couldn't eat a whole one, as the joke goes. Well, I couldn't anyway. I'm not about to eat them raw and I've only got a small cooker which can barely fit a 3lb turkey. Anyway, as I was saying, kids... They come in various different shapes and sizes (none of which fit very well into an oven), but one thing's true about them all: They've got very squeaky voices.

Eventually, of course, boys' voices break. It happens earlier for some than others – there's always one scarily overdeveloped lad in the class who sings tenor, has a moustache and gets married just before his tenth birthday. This is the same guy who scrawled 'inches' in biro on the bottom of his 'I AM 9' badge. Equally, there are some unfortunates whose voice never descends, for whatever reason. It might be genetics. Or it might be the Raleigh Chopper.

The Chopper was the bicycle of the late 1970s that everyone wanted to own. It was so cool, like one of those motorbikes out of *Easy Rider*. But with pedals. And playing cards wedged between the spokes of the wheels so it made a rattling noise as you pedalled along (I'll bet Dennis Hopper wishes he'd thought of that).

Raleigh's bike also boasted a larger back wheel, and hence a heavy rear end which made it easy to pull wheelies. In fact the only time you rode about on two wheels was when you were pedalling like mad to get home in time for your tea. In theory, it was the perfect poseur's stunt bike, but the Chopper held a deadly secret.

Well, two deadly secrets. The first was that if you did ride it fast, it started to wobble. This wasn't just a slight swaying either – this was pure mad wobbling, like an epileptic Weeble on top of a washing machine on full spin cycle. Fortunately, the damn thing weighed so much that actually getting speed up was nearly impossible without the help of a steep slope.

So that wasn't the real danger. That lay in the infamous chunky gear lever, positioned along the top of the frame, just in front of the seat. The upshot of this design was that if you braked too hard, you slid off the seat and damn nearly split your knacker-sack on the bastard thing. Chopper by name, and chopper by nature, it really should have been called the Eunuch-Maker. Although I suspect that might have had something of a negative impact on sales, a bit like renaming Black Pudding "Clotted Pig's Blood" or 4x4s "Wanker Trucks".

So the next time you meet a bloke with an unnaturally squeaky voice, spare a moment to think about the crippling bike accident he likely had as a kid. And if you're a woman, try to avoid asking for a go on his chopper. That's probably still a sore point.

Probably the most dangerous bike in the world.

Clackers

The Nintendo DS of the early 1970s, Clackers were essentially two hard plastic balls attached by string to a ring that the player inserted his or her finger into (the sexual connotations were rife). The idea was to move your hand up and down, which caused the balls to swing apart and back together, clacking when they collided.

And that was it. THAT WAS IT. Jesus. At least there was some vague point to the hula hoop (it allowed you to watch Cathy Bates's boobs swing from side to side during break-time) and the pogo stick (it allowed you to watch Cathy Bates's boobs bounce up and down during break-time) but Clackers were shit. If you were very good, you could get the balls clacking in an arc above and below your hand, which introduced an element of danger to the proceedings. You could clout your fingers, give yourself a dead wrist, or the balls could shatter and possibly have someone's eye out, which seems a fitting punishment for playing the stupid game in the first place.

The daft things were eventually banned for safety reasons. Presumably when debating whether or not to prohibit Clackers, the teachers asked the children for a show of hands… and the bruised knuckles, wrists and fingers they saw carried the motion unanimously.

The Clangers

We are not alone. There's life on distant planets. It's made of wool and it whistles? Fuck off.

Colour-changing T-shirts

It was a technological breakthrough poised to revolutionize the clothes industry: T-shirts that changed colour based on your body temperature. When you got warm, the fabric turned a different hue. Fantastic. The problem was it only changed colour where you were hottest, like under your armpits. So rather than being a clever, cutting-edge piece of fashionwear, the shirts only served to make you look like a sweaty fucker. Which, for some reason, didn't go down that well with the fickle buying public.

A shame really, as if they had been a major success we could doubtless have looked forward to other items of colour-changing clothing in a similar vein. Swimsuits that changed from white to bright yellow in the presence of urine for example, or trousers designed to turn a fetching shade of brown around the arse every time you farted. Never mind starving themselves before a fashion show, models would have been forced to adopt a whole new eating regime, downing pints of water and tucking into baked beans and cabbage before taking to the catwalk. This "Pret-a-Farter" range could have gone down a storm – or at the very least been as noisy as one.

Corona
Drink popular around 1975–79

Before any bubbles could get into a bottle of this popular 1970s soft drink – available in lemonade, orangeade, limeade and dandelion and burdock flavours – they first had to pass a "fizzical". This get fit process was overseen, in the adverts at least, by a Sergeant Bilko-esque giant bubble who motivated them with lines such as "C'mon, c'mon, c'mon, move, move, move!" and "Ah, that's it boys, let's see you fizz, fizz, fizz!"

Presumably it was the high-powered exercise routine the bubbles had to endure that gave every variant of Corona a taste akin to fizzy sweat.

Crackerjack
TV Programme popular around 1960–84

Introduced with the spine-chilling phrase "It's Friday, it's five to five… It's *Crackerjack!*" this kids' TV programme ran for nearly 30 years and was hosted by a wide range of presenters. The names read like a roll call of the worst in showbiz – Ed "Stewpot" Stewart, Peter Glaze, Don Maclean, Bernie Clifton, The Krankies, Ronnie Corbett…

Unquestionably the shittest of them all was Stu Francis, who presented *Crackerjack* from 1979 to 1984. He had a range of catchphrases which were actually more just phrases, seeing as they were never going to catch on. "Ooh, I could crush a grape", "Ooh, I could jump off a doll's house", "Ooh, I could rip a tissue." In truth Stu was so wet he probably couldn't do any of those things. The real catchphrase from the show was actually its name. The mere mention of the word *"Crackerjack"* would lead to the audience yelling it back at ear-splitting volume.

The programme offered a mixture of games for kids (with the legendary *Crackerjack* pencil as a consolation prize), music and variety acts. Highlights included a comedy double act – although Peter Glaze and Don Maclean were more of a tragedy double act – and Double or Drop, a game in which kids were asked questions and given a prize to hold for every answer they got right, and a cabbage for every incorrect response. The game continued with items being piled ever higher until the contestant dropped one. Eating all those cabbages afterwards would have led to the whole family "dropping one", I'd have thought.

At some point in the show, Bernie Clifton would "ride" in on the back of his ostrich, Oswald. Much hilarity would ensue. In his mind, at least.

The programme was incredibly popular and in our house we only had to hear those introductory words "It's Friday, it's five to five..." and we'd all rush to the telly. The faster the channel was changed, the better for everyone.

Crowded House — Pop Group popular around 1986–96

There have been plenty of ironically named pop groups, but Crowded House were one of the front-runners in this department. If you played their music at a house party, the place wouldn't likely be crowded. There'd be a mass exodus to the chip shop before you could say "Who put this shit on?"

The Crystal Maze — TV Programme popular around 1990–95

The Crystal Maze was a game show in which six middle-management yuppie prats, complete with power hairdos and posh accents, battled against fiendish mental puzzles, exacting tests of skill and gruelling physical tasks. Well, they were piss-easy really, but the contestants made them look hard. In all honesty, the most gruelling thing about going on the show should've been having to put up with the hyperactive bald host Richard O'Brien (of *Rocky Horror* fame) prattling on like an incessant wind-bag.

You see, while the players were tackling the short games in an effort to win crystals, there were occasional periods of silence which he had to fill with something. He could always play his harmonica or talk about his mum ("mumsy") but when he'd run out of his stock gags, he was forced to start yammering on about his cat wallpapering his lounge or some other load of old bollocks.

But even that wasn't half as irritating as watching the contestants attempt to complete the challenges against the clock. Generally, the puzzles were very simple and every viewer could see what needed to be done. For example, there would be some wooden shapes on the floor, and a picture of a cube on the wall showing that you had to fit the shapes together to construct a cube.

Cue the typical blockhead of a contestant. They would enter the puzzle room, and maniacally begin to shout "What do I do? What do I do?" while dashing around looking confused, before suddenly spotting the picture of the cube and trying to prise it off the wall to see if the crystal was hidden behind it. They would fail miserably because it was nailed firmly up, so then they'd ask their team-mates if anyone could see a crowbar, then scrabble about in the sawdust that covered the floor trying to find a crowbar. Then they'd spot the wooden shapes, pick the longest and thinnest one up and attempt to use that as a crowbar to lever the cube picture off the wall again. They'd fail miserably, fail to hear their team-mates telling them they only have ten seconds left because they're still screaming "What do I do?" loudly, then finally dash to the exit door with one second remaining on the clock only to have it slammed in their face by Richard and get locked in.

Most of the challenges went something like this, until the programme makers relented and wheeled out the stupidly easy no-fail affairs they'd adapted from primary school games – put the square peg in the square-shaped hole, put the star peg in the star-shaped hole... That ensured the team won at least a couple of crystals and thus a little time in the crystal dome.

This wasn't a Swarovski replica of O'Brien's head, but a grandiosely named plastic bubble in which the end game was played. This involved a giant fan (surely the only one of the show) blowing gold and silver foil tokens in the air. The contestants had to collect the gold tokens by jumping up and grabbing them, while avoiding the silver ones. To make it even trickier, it was difficult to breathe in the dome, what with the amount of hairspray cloying the atmosphere from all those bouffant do's being wildly blown about.

At the end of this humiliating ordeal, they'd invariably attain a negative score from having more silver than gold, and Richard (or host of the later shows Ed Tudor-Pole) would present them with a small crystal trophy upon which was engraved the legend "I cracked the Crystal Maze." Even though they'd lost abysmally and blatantly couldn't crack an egg between them.

Deeley Boppers — Novelty popular around 1975–85

When work's Christmas do comes around, there's always the danger that someone a little bit wacky – usually from the IT department – will turn up wearing something a little *different*. These days, it might be a *Comic Relief* red nose, or perhaps one of those shirts with a scrolling LED message (hopefully "Please punch me in the face"). In the past, however, the thoroughbred office tosser would arrive sporting a pair of tinsel entwined Deeley Boppers.

The humble Deeley Bopper would make the wearer look crazy MAD. People would know they were MAD because they were wearing a headband with two springs attached, on the end of which were a couple of plastic or fluffy balls, which wobbled about and made them look MAD. Not only MAD, but also SAD and DANGEROUS TO KNOW, or even DANGEROUS TO STAND NEAR IN A BUS QUEUE just in case someone mistook you and the unhinged Bopper enthusiast as possible acquaintances.

With their funky alien antennae appearance, a set of Deeleys certainly made you look like you'd come from another planet – a far-flung long lost world which time might not have quite forgotten, but taste definitely had.

Someone call the NSPCC, and quick.

Designer Stubble — Fashionable Look popular around 1985–90

Too lazy to shave? That's okay – it's the height of fashion! Popularized by Don Johnson on *Miami Vice* and George Michael post-Wham, having a five o'clock shadow in the 1980s no longer made you look scruffy, it made you look stylish. Whoever coined the phrase "designer stubble" was a genius. What a shame they didn't apply the "designer" prefix to other examples of slothful unsanitary behaviour.

Not cleaned your teeth for a few days? That's fine – it's designer halitosis! Been wearing the same underpants for a fortnight or longer? Revel in your designer skidmarks! People turning their noses up at you because you haven't washed for a month? Put them straight, that's not B.O. they can smell – it's designer pheromones!

That man sleeping rough in a doorway? He's not an alcoholic Glaswegian tramp,

he's a designer indigent. And look, you can tell how fashionable he is. He's designer pissed himself.

Dirty Dancing

If you're a woman you probably loved this film when it came out. If you're a (straight) man you won't ever have watched it, or if you did you'll have scratched your head afterwards and wondered what all the fuss was about.

Dirty Dancing starred Patrick Swayze as dance instructor Johnny Castle and Jennifer Grey as Frances "Baby" Houseman. The plot basically revolves around Johnny's dance partner getting pregnant, Baby standing in for her, and her and Johnny falling in love. Baby pays for Johnny's partner to have an abortion which goes wrong, and everyone thinks Johnny's the father – he isn't – which leads to universal disapproval. The young lovers are forced to keep their romance a secret, but eventually the truth comes out, there's a big old dance scene at the end and then Schwarzenegger arrives with an Uzi and guns down the pathetic lot of them. (If only).

There's plenty of dancing throughout the film, all set to a soundtrack you frankly won't have been able to avoid even if you were dead, and at some point in the movie Patrick Swayze says "Nobody puts Baby in a corner," and all the girls in the audience swoon. Clint Eastwood was later to disprove this statement when he won an Oscar for his boxing flick which put a *Million Dollar Baby* in a corner.

Any men foolish enough to have agreed to watch the film with their girlfriend/wife will, at this point, receive an undisguised look of withering disappointment simply for failing to be Patrick Swayze. The men will be equally disappointed, however, because by now it's abundantly clear that the dancing is indeed the dirtiest thing about the movie, and it's not even performed naked.

The film was the best-selling video of the time and the soundtrack shifted zillions of copies. No doubt Kleenex flogged a load of tissues too, as they were especially needed at the point where someone tries to put Baby in a corner and a dance instructor won't let him/her/it. Whatever.

Patrick sang one of the songs in the film, "She's Like The Wind". And indeed, if she was like the wind, this film was like the follow-through.

Let's be honest. *Doctor Who* was always rubbish, wasn't it? Not so much now, obviously, with its more grown-up relationship themes and computer generated effects. But back in its heyday of the 1970s and 1980s, it was incredibly amateurish stuff.

Ever wondered why the Daleks became the Doctor's number one enemy? Why people took to them more than any other foe? Because they were believable. Sure, they looked like giant pepper pots, couldn't climb stairs, were easy to outrun, didn't have hands, and probably lacked any depth of vision due to only having that one eye on a stalk... but at least they didn't look like a bunch of men wearing cheap latex costumes and papier mâché masks. Unlike 95% of the rest of the creatures the Doctor encountered.

Daleks could conquer any planet. Provided the disabled facilities were OK.

The show's special effects were far from special. You needed a vivid imagination to dream for one second that the Doctor and his various assistants were in any danger from enemies like the Bacofoil Cybermen or the frying pan lid toting Sea Devils. When you take into account the Daleks' kitchen sink plunger appendages, it becomes clear that the BBC canteen was a great source of props for the show.

A rogue Timelord – the Master – was one of the more convincing antagonists the Doctor came up against, but only because he was supposed to look human and didn't require any ridiculous makeup. Although the poor sod still got lumbered with a goatee beard that appeared to have been hastily ripped from a pretend cave-girl's nether regions and stuck on with double-sided Sellotape.

The low budget didn't apply solely to the monsters – everything was done on the cheap. The TARDIS looked as if it was constructed from industrial strength balsa wood. Sturdy enough to travel through time and space? Sure, provided no one bumped into it and there wasn't any wind blowing. If it looked much larger on the inside than the outside, that's probably because the moment you went through the door it fell apart, leaving you standing foolishly in a large open space surrounded by four collapsed walls.

As for the acting, that was often more wooden than the furniture. To be fair though, in some cases that was because the furniture was made from distressed sticky-back plastic. The plots were no help – they had more holes in them than Tom Baker's colourful loose knit scarf.

When *Doctor Who* was on the telly there was only one place to view it and that was from behind the sofa. Not because the show was scary, but because it was so embarrassing you simply couldn't bear to watch every time the Doctor found himself being menaced by a plague victim with teabag boils or a giant robot constructed from what looked suspiciously like used cutlery.

"Do They Know It's Christmas?" — Song popular around 1984–89

Band Aid's 1984 Christmas number one featured the vocal talents of everyone from Boy George and George Michael to Paul Weller and Bono. It became the fastest and biggest selling single of the decade and, thanks to subsequent re-recordings, re-releases and concerts, raised a staggering amount of money for the famine hit areas of Africa. There's no questioning the positive impact Bob Geldof and Midge Ure's charity juggernaut had, or the number of lives that it saved. Which is fantastic.

A shame then that the actual record itself was shit. A total crap-fest with some of the worst, most embarrassing lyrics ever penned. Here are a few of them to cringe along with:

"And there won't be snow in Africa this Christmas time."

Ignoring the drifts up in the mountains, this line is spot on. There won't. What with Christmas falling in the middle of summer over there, and it being an equatorial continent and all. Similarly, there won't be a beach volleyball competition in Antarctica this winter-time.

"Do they know it's Christmas time at all?"

More to the point, given their plight, do they actually give a shit?

"Here's to you, raise a glass for everyone. Here's to them, underneath that burning sun."

Oh yes. Let's raise a glass of freshly-popped Bolly to the poor, starving inhabitants of a continent where millions of people have no or limited access to clean drinking water. They'll really appreciate the gesture. Everyone loves displays of moneyed excess! The bread-demanding peasants of France just loved it when Marie Antoinette raised her plate of Black Forest Gateaux to them. It was a real riot.

"Feed the world. Let them know it's Christmas time."

How exactly? By sending the starving people of Africa cooked turkeys, Christmas puddings, mince pies, crackers and party hats? Or maybe Band Aid could send a jolly fat old man with a bushy white beard to deliver sacks of grain in a reindeer powered sledge?

After Band Aid came Live Aid. The global concert is seen as one of the defining moments of the 1980s. Who can forget the end of the gig when the stage filled with generations of performers, joining in on the famous song's chorus, telling the viewing billions we should feed the world and let them know it was Christmas time. Even though it blatantly wasn't. We watched as they cheerfully sang their crappy and wholly inappropriate yuletide ditty on that balmy July night and, with the festive bells chiming along, we thanked God it was them, instead of us, making utter tits of themselves.

Dragon's Lair — Video Game popular around 1983–87

These days we're pretty blasé about computer games with cartoon-quality graphics, but in the early 1980s blocky pixels was as good as it got. Then Dragon's Lair arrived. Created by former Disney animator Don Bluth, it looked just like a Disney cartoon. The first time you ever saw Dragon's Lair you were rendered utterly speechless. A bit like the first time Cathy Bates showed you her lady bits round the back of the bike shed.

You could tell which arcades had just managed to get hold of the new machine by the massive queue of eager kids stretching all the way back to Woollies. Every skiving child as desperate as the next to step into the shoes of Dirk the Daring and rescue Princess Daphne from Singe, the evil dragon, while avoiding perilous pitfalls (and double maths). It looked amazing and as for the game play…

Well, there wasn't any.

To "play" the game, you simply had to move the joystick in a certain direction, or press the sword button at the correct moment. Easy enough, except you had to do it with a precision more accurate than the speaking clock. Being attacked? Press sword. Oops too late. Falling down a well on a large wooden platform? Better press forward then. Nope, wrong timing. Being swept down a river of lava? Quick go right. No left. Not now. NOW! Oh fuck it. It required a massive amount of skill, luck and good judgement, but mostly it required a massive amount of ten pence pieces. Dragon's Lair was a bit like an electronic version of the school bully, as it took all your lunch money and then laughed at you for being useless; the only meaningful distinction being that you got to prod a stick occasionally, instead of being prodded by a stick occasionally. Which of course made all the difference.

Dr Seuss — Books popular around 1960–80

Dr Seuss wrote silly rhymes,
Was that really such a crime?
Yes, because they ne'er made sense,
Now lick your foot twice with a fence.
He wrote of cats, in hats, on mats,
He wrote until his books got fat,
He wrote of ham and green eggs too,
He wrote while he sat on the loo.
And how can we be sure of this?
Because he wrote a load of shit.

Dungeons & Dragons — Game popular around 1980-2000

Dungeons & Dragons, or D&D as it's commonly abbreviated, is a role-playing game which became really popular around 1980. Normal children would go off to play with their friends, but then return as if possessed, bragging about how they'd conquered the Keep on the Borderlands, and slaughtered 50 of the Dungeon Master's goblins with a "Finger of Death" spell.

Naturally, parents became alarmed by these odd sounding violent tales, and the source of all this disturbing imagination, D&D, was linked to witchcraft and Satanism by some excitable types. It has to be said though, anyone who thought playing that particular game would turn teenagers into devil worshippers really didn't know much about it. A simple séance would have taken ages to complete: "You roll a 4. The glass moves to M. If you roll a 1 or 3 you can challenge someone you suspect of having pushed it. If you roll any other number, you must roll again to see where the glass moves next."

A demon summoning would've been even worse: "You need to draw a pentagram. First you must procure the blood chalk of Demogorgon to etch it with, which is held in a magical prism by the Archmage Lasiien, who resides in the Plane of Pandemonium, which is reached by a teleport spell that's scribed on a unique parchment, the scroll of Xerthik, last seen in the ancient library of the town of Nathri'kt, which is in the province of..."

For those who never experienced D&D, the game was run by one person called the Dungeon Master (DM) who controlled all the monsters and other characters in the game world. The DM wielded supreme power and sat behind a cardboard screen cackling to himself, looking at a multitude of charts and rolling various dice to decide the outcome of everything.

The players assumed various different roles. There was the fighter who hit things, the thief who nicked things, the cleric who healed things, and the wizard who was completely useless. He had a paltry amount of hit-points (health), meaning that he risked death facing, say, a particularly stiff breeze, and he could only manage to cast one spell every three weeks or so. After his magic was spent, he was reduced to cowering in the back ranks and firing a catapult at monsters, which, if he was lucky enough to roll a natural 20, could quite savagely graze a troll's elbow. A mage who lived long enough to attain a high level could actually become very powerful, although that was an unlikely occurrence to say the least. If you played by the rules he had the same odds of survival as a barbecue-sauce-smeared seal in a polar bear's den.

Just as well, then, that the majority of players cheated and fudged like a government statistician, and everyone ended up with a near-invincible thirtieth level hero. This might have helped considerably in the game, but sadly these powers never translated into real life.

A million gold pieces wouldn't buy you anything from the tuck shop, and neither could you teleport out of the clutches of the school bully. And the nearest you could get to a "Finger of Death" spell was a Finger of Fudge, which might have been chock full of Cadbury goodness, but it didn't have quite the same effect when flung at your maths teacher.

Duran Duran — Pop Group popular around 1981–85

Duran Duran were the most successful of the New Romantic bands – which

Tragedy and comedy blended in a manner that Shakespeare could only dream of.

basically means they wore the most foundation and used the most hair products on their ridiculously bouffant hairdo's. The band's dressing room was guaranteed to be chock-full of aerosols. And cans of hairspray.

They did also sell the most records, true, although you do have to wonder how. It must have been those much vaunted videos such as the one for "The Reflex". This contained a momentous scene where a vast wall of water cascades from a video screen over a crowd of adoring fans, a cutting-edge special effect at the time, which now unfortunately looks like a superimposed child's doodle in blue crayon.

Sadly, all this contemporary technical wizardry was ever so slightly ruined when the director cut to a close-up of the crowd and got a passing window cleaner to chuck his bucket of suds over them. That was supposed to represent the crashing home of this Hawaii Five-O sized monster surf wave?

But at least they had those great lyrics. Like the song "Rio", which went:

"Her name is Rio and she dances on the sands/Just like that river twisting through a dusty land."

Yes, forget summer days, what girls really want to be compared to is rivers – "Let me compare thee to the River Thames: thou art slightly fishy and full of shit." Maybe they were just trying to say they got women wet. Which I suppose they did. In "The Reflex" video anyway.

However, the classic "Rio" line was:

"It means so much to me; Like a birthday or a pretty view."

All of Duran Duran were credited with writing this song, and that's what their collectively pooled minds came up with? Fuck knows what it would have turned out like if one of them had to think up the lyrics on their own. ("Rio saw the ball, Rio threw the ball. Run, Rio, Run!").

Another famous song was: "(Please, Please, Tell Me Now) Is There Something I Should Know?" Yes, there is. You're shit. You were shit at your height and you still are today. Their line-up has occasionally changed over the years, but the band endures and we appear to have to endure them as well. Still, there's no question I prefer the contemporary Duran Duran. Primarily because they are much easier to totally avoid. It's not like they're actually played on the radio or anything.

Eldorado — TV Programme popular around 1992–93

The legendary Eldorado was a lost city of gold. Its namesake, which replaced *Wogan* on BBC1 in the 1990s, was more of a Spanish resort of shit. The soap opera followed the lives of a bunch of ex-pats in Spain's Los Barcos, and should have been a massive success with its blend of sun, sex and sangria.

Unfortunately, there were just a couple of teensy-weensy things wrong with it. Nothing major. Just trivial affairs like, oh I dunno, most of the cast being unable to act, the scripts being rubbish, and sound that echoed so badly it was hard to understand what the characters were saying at times. Mind you, that was true without the echoing too, as some of the dialogue was unwisely spoken in various European languages. Without subtitles. It was embarrassing, it was amateurish and it made you long for the return of *Wogan*. Yes, it was *that* bad. On the plus side, at least *Eldorado* was only half an hour long.

There were some memorable characters, such as Marcus Tandy who ended up stealing the show. Partly because he was convincingly acted, and therefore stood out, and also because he had a tasty girlfriend called Pilar (nice). Then there was teenage bride Fizz, the girl married to Bunny – or "Booneh" as she called him – who was routinely acted off the screen by concrete pillars.

The rest of the cast were a mixed bunch. There was a disabled girl, a gay guy, two (not so great) Danes and, naturally, various Spanish people, although not one of the locals was called Manuel or Jose. With that poor level of realism, it's no wonder the BBC pulled the plug on the soap after just a year.

Etch-a-Sketch

The Etch-a-Sketch first became really popular in the 1960s. It was a doodling toy which featured a screen with two twiddly knobs underneath it. When you turned the knobs, you drew lines on the screen. Wow! Like magic!

On the adverts, they always showed some youthful Da Vinci-wannabe etching out a pretty convincing rendition of The Last Supper, but the reality of the toy was that it was pretty bloody difficult to draw anything except a straight line. Even something as simple as a diagonal was tricky, as you had to turn both knobs at *precisely* the same speed, which meant that most kids ended up drawing pictures of roofless houses. Otherwise known as squares.

The Etch-a-Sketch, or as it was known in our house, the Bore-a-Draw.

Instead of splashing out on this expensive plastic box, you could have dug out a piece of paper and a pencil and obtained more impressive results for free. Having said that, the device did have its uses. When faced with a pair of naked breasts for the first time, the ardent Etch-a-Sketcher knew exactly what to do with those nipples.

Evel Knievel Stunt Cycle

Evel was a big hero in the 1970s, yet we never found out why he was evil, and we also never found out why he couldn't spell. He constantly wowed kids and adults alike with his daring stunts, even though he regularly ballsed them up and came a cropper.

For example, there was the time he failed to jump thirteen buses at Wembley in 1975. To be fair, that many double-deckers was a very difficult jump to make, and not just because the distance involved in clearing them was considerable. The really tricky bit was getting the buses to all turn up at the same time, given the fundamental rule of the bus drivers' charter that roughly half of buses turn up early, half late, and one mysteriously never arrives at all.

It was a thrill to watch Knievel jump as a kid, but an even bigger thrill to recreate his feats with the Evel Knievel Stunt Cycle and some dinky toy buses.

The Stunt Cycle consisted of a model motorbike ridden by an Evel doll, plus a crank device which powered it up. You cranked and cranked, then cranked some more, charging the bike up before letting it rip onto a ring binder or other improvised ramp and watching as Evel soared through the air and landed perfectly. Yeah right.

What was more likely is you'd crank and wind and crank so hard your hand would slip, scraping the skin off your knuckles on the concrete floor of the garage, which was the only place you were allowed to play with the thing since

Crank once. Crank twice. Crank bike.

Evel smacked square into mum's shin and made her spill tea down her favourite dress. The bike would then fly off the crude ramp at an angle and hit the wall, and a bit of it would break off, usually the handlebars. Which was a definite reversal compared to real life, where it was bits of Evel that would generally snap.

There were accessories you could buy alongside the Stunt Cycle, such as Evel's Stunt Truck complete with a proper ramp – not that this made much difference to the accuracy of his jumps. He still dented polished pine skirting boards in homes across the country, until he was banned from the house. The extreme winding-up that the cycle got was nothing on what poor old mum had to suffer.

Fake Ice Cubes   Practical Joke popular around 1970–80

The absolutely height of hilarity, the novelty ice cube was the inimitable prank which was just unutterably funny and guaranteed to liven up any dinner. Waiter, waiter, there's a fly in my ice cube! Wait a minute – it's not an ice cube after all! It's a clear plastic cube with a pretend fly in it, that one of my friends has placed there in an unprecedented stroke of comic genius! Ha ha!

The really funny thing, however, is that it would probably have been more hygienic to put a real fly in there. Back in the 1970s, safety was a word which only applied to pins, and the plastic cubes were probably more toxic than a polonium sales conference.

Fantasy Island   TV Programme popular around 1978–84

This long-running television series was set on an island in the Pacific that people could hire to live out their fantasies. It was a bit like a big budget fictional version of *Jim'll Fix It*, and it even had its very own creepy old man running the show – the spooky Mr Roarke.

The island's guests were a mixed bunch. There were amnesiacs hoping to regain their memories, rich people wanting to be liked for themselves and not just their money, parents desperate to meet the children they gave up for adoption, and would-be detectives looking to solve crimes… All totally shit fantasies in other words. In over seven series, not one person turned up at the island having requested five naked Miss Worlds, ten gallons of baby oil, and a bouncy castle. Just ridiculous.

The guests all arrived by plane, and we knew they were on their way when Tattoo, Mr Roarke's diminutive assistant, started ringing a bell and dementedly shouting "Da plane, da plane," from the top of a tower. It was an amusing catchphrase initially, but it soon grated. No doubt Mr Roarke's fantasy was to bury the annoying little tosser head first in the sand and wait for the tide to come in. But if you've ever got absolutely bladdered on a night out and woken up in the morning to discover David and Victoria Beckham etched on your arse cheeks (Victoria could probably fit in the crack), you'll know just how hard it is to get rid of an unwanted tattoo.

The dwarf did vanish towards the end of the show's life though, replaced by a butler who rang the Island's bell simply by pressing a button. Viewers responded to the casting change by pressing buttons of their own. Ones marked off.

Femidom   Prophylactic popular around 1992–97

Despite sounding like a robot dominatrix, the Femidom was in fact a female contraceptive. In less enlightened countries, where men consider wearing condoms during sex to be about as enticing a proposition as wearing a bear trap, the product became extremely popular and indeed is often considered a lifesaver. When it was introduced to the UK in the early 1990s, it met with an equally enthusiastic reception. We all whooped, clapped and laughed at it.

Not surprising really. It was certainly a funny looking thing. The advertising campaign announced that "Johnny's had a sex change," presumably to Joanie, but not only had it changed sex, it had changed size too. It looked like a pair of diaphragms attached to a regular condom that had been used as a water balloon, then stretched over someone's head and inflated in a comedy fashion during a particularly raucous party. Which it possibly had.

Slipping a condom on can be tricky at times, especially if you've had a few and brewer's droop has come into play, but putting a Femidom in was far more awkward. It pretty much involved the woman having to fist herself, which isn't something many ladies would like to be seen doing in front of a regular sexual partner, let alone one they've just met. For this reason alone, it was the perfect form of protection. Removing a sexy woman's knickers and discovering a penis would probably be less off-putting than watching her stuff what appeared to be a large carrier bag up her vagina. And if she did it in the bathroom beforehand, you'd be forgiven for thinking you'd pulled John Wayne when she eventually came waddling seductively out.

However, couples looking to spice up their sex lives might have found it an invaluable tool. He could wear a pilot's uniform, and she could join in the aeronautical theme by lying back and pretending to be a windsock.

The Femidom didn't just look ridiculous, it sounded it too. If you videoed yourself having sex it would provide the perfect soundtrack for the movie by rustling loudly, just as if someone was ferreting around in the bottom of a near-empty bag of popcorn during a night out at the pictures.

It wasn't so much a passion killer as a passion slaughterer. Having sex with a woman wearing one was like fucking a bin liner – it brought new meaning to the phrase "rubbish shag." In its short and not entirely best-selling time on the shelves, the Femidom did manage to reduce the spread of sexually transmitted diseases amongst women who wore one. Presumably this wasn't due to its contraceptive powers, but more to the fact that most men who encountered one in the wilds – or , as the Aussies say, in the Bush – decided feigning a headache was the safest course of action.

Fighting Fantasy — Books popular around 1982–90

The Fighting Fantasy series might sound like a collection of depraved violent bondage videos, but they were actually books based on role-playing games. No, not the kind of role-playing which involves nurse uniforms, but the Dungeons & Dragons craze of the mid-1980s.

The idea of the books like *The Warlock of Firetop Mountain* was that the hero was YOU (I've no idea why they always put that in capitals, probably to make YOU feel important). YOU made the decisions as YOU raided the Warlock's dungeon of traps and monsters, seeking to plunder his treasure. Like a common thief. Never mind rap music, how many kids set off on the road to a life of crime and burglary after reading Firetop Mountain?

The Fighting Fantasy books were conceived by Steve Jackson and Ian Livingstone. They were divided into 400 sections, numbered 1 to 400, although later in the series they expanded them further. You began at number 1 and after reading the text, you were offered several options and had to choose one, then turn to that number. At times you'd have to fight monsters using dice rolls, or make "skill checks" to achieve certain feats. It all went a little something like this:

[1]

You walk into a cavern. The air is thick and musty with the stench of goblins. The little green bleeders must have cooked up a curry last night. Your eyes adjust to the darkness and you spy some pallid white mushrooms on the floor near the cavern walls. There are two passageways, one to the East which slopes downwards where the musty smell seems to be emanating from, and one to the North.

Turn to 21 if you head North.

Turn to 56 if you head East.

Turn to 83 if you pick a mushroom and eat it.

[21]

You walk down the North passageway. It gets wider as you travel along it and the heavy clanking footsteps of your plate-mail boots echo ominously. You reach a T-junction. You wonder what you are doing with your life. Perhaps if you went outside and played footy with the rest of your schoolmates they wouldn't call you speccy-piss-pants-sad-act.

Turn to 188 if you head right.

Turn to 229 if you head left.

[56]

What are you, some sort of idiot? East is where the goblin smell's coming from, dumbo. And it slopes downwards, quite clearly suggesting things are going to go downhill. You berk. You enter a room full of goblin warriors and they rip you to pieces, dance on your jibbly bits and then nominate you for a Darwin award.

The End.

[83]

You tentatively pluck a mushroom from the cavern floor and eat it. Everything goes a bit wobbly and funny, but not in a good way.

Turn to Page 1 of *Fear and Loathing in Las Vegas* by Hunter S Thompson (quest for a copy in the Labyrinth of Dad's Bookshelf).

[188]

You walk down the right passage. As you travel along, it changes from natural rock to shaped and clearly man-made walls. There are lit alcoves spaced at regular intervals containing ornate vases. It's a very pleasant hallway. Suddenly a skeleton jumps out of an alcove ahead and waves a large two-handed sword around menacingly. You wonder how a skeleton can lift a big hunk of metal when it doesn't have any muscles, then you crack a joke about crash diets.

If you charge at the skeleton with your shield, turn to… etc…

[229]

You walk down the left passageway. Nothing much happens. It's a very drab and dull passage. You walk a bit more. It's pretty boring really. Still nothing doing. You're now thinking about the right passageway, aren't you? And how much better it might be? Don't even think about flicking back to 21 and choosing to go the other way. The Warlock will see your cheating, he knows all and he'll curse your offspring so they have extremely small genitalia. You eventually reach the end of the turgid passageway. Shake the dice and roll less than your LUCK skill or fall asleep. Forever. It's one of those magic sleeps.

If you're still awake, turn to… etc…

First Generation VCRs   Electrical Goods popular around 1978–85

When video recorders were first launched, they were a status symbol. Only the well-off could afford a VCR to tape *Coronation Street* on a Monday night. Of course, the well-off wouldn't have been taping *Corrie*, it would have been more likely to be *Panorama* or *Newsnight* – which is a bit like owning one of the first vibrators ever invented and using it to stir your tea.

Despite being cutting-edge electronics at the time, the original VCRs were huge silvery grey breezeblocks with clunky top-loading tape mechanisms and this amazing feature called "tracking." This was a dial that tuned the picture and removed any flaws or noise you might encounter when using an older tape (or one you'd bought down the market out of a suitcase).

That was the theory, anyway. In actual fact, this fine-tuning process turned into a fun game of move the interference around. You could have flickering lines of interference at the top of the screen, or at the bottom, or in the middle. With the

The quality of early recordings meant every tape was a video nasty.

power of tracking, the choice was yours. But you could never, ever, actually get rid of the sodding picture noise.

There were two types of video recorder in these early days, VHS and Betamax. Most people bought VHS and it quickly became the dominant format. The fact that the early porn barons chose VHS might have had something to do with its success.

Poor old Betamax owners became a laughing stock, almost social lepers. A stray finger plopping in your soup at a dinner party would probably have raised less eyebrows than admitting you owned a Betamax video recorder. VHS owners, on the other hand, didn't have to worry about injured pride. Just injured wrists after their ninth viewing of *Electric Blue 26*.

Flares

Clothes popular around 1960–80

Not the pyrotechnic illumination devices, but the exceptionally baggy trousers that became popular in the 1960s and 1970s. I'm sure there hasn't ever been a more stupid invention in the fashion world – even including the concept catwalk stuff like lampshade dresses made out of tin foil with bin liner straps, and hats made from peacock's nipples. All right, so the design theory of flares is sort of sound, to a point. Tight trousers can make you sweat, especially in hotter weather, and they can be uncomfortable, possibly even crushing/cutting into your bits. So there's nothing wrong with a pair of airy jeans, but at what point did some fashion guru wanker decide that 20-inch bellbottoms were going to sell? Around the same time that LSD became really popular, I reckon, which must also be the reason why they did start selling in some sort of quantity. Hippies really have a lot to answer for.

Bellbottoms weren't merely airy in the leg, they comprised of a cavernous expanse of canvas the same size as your average hot air balloon. If you ever do wear a pair – say you're going to a fancy dress party, or maybe you've just gone mental – be very careful not to walk over any Marilyn Monroe style grates in the pavement, or you might find yourself launched off into the stratosphere on an impromptu Phileas Fogg expedition. Incidentally, they were called bellbottoms because they're shaped to look like a large bell where the trousers end. Funnily enough, the wearer looked like a large bell end too. Coincidence? I think not.

Not only do huge flares look ridiculous, but they're uncomfortable as well. When walking, the excess material on each leg flaps together, so it's like riding along on a couple of heavy fluttering flags. And the static electricity build-up, for those with nylon carpets, can be massive and potentially lethal. It's a little known fact that energy saving pioneers researched using flared trousers as an alternative power source. Sadly, solar flares never took off.

Perhaps the most unbelievable thing about flares is that they made a big comeback in the 1990s. Which just goes to show that if the clothes buying public was told that the inflated bladder from a freshly slaughtered sheep was this winter's trendy headgear of choice, come Christmas the entire country would be parading around with mutton piss dribbling down their necks.

More a fashion suicide note than a fashion statement.

Flight Deck

Toy popular around 1973–76

Toys used to be much simpler in the old days. Forget Playstations, Robosapiens and Lego Mindstorms. In the early 1970s all kids wanted for Christmas was a Flight Deck from Airfix. This toy consisted of a control panel that looked as if it had been ripped straight from a fighter plane cockpit, a scale model plastic aircraft carrier and a matching F4 Phantom plane.

The telly adverts made it look as if the plane could really fly – but that was a large fib. What it could do, just about, was slide down a piece of fishing wire. The joystick gave you some minor control over its positioning and when it got to the carrier, the plane would catch on a small piece of line stretched across the deck and a flag would pop up to indicate a successful landing. You then pulled the plane back up the fishing wire, let it go and watched as it slid down again. And when it had landed once more you left it alone and went off to play with something much more fun. Like the empty box.

In 1975, Airfix returned to the drawing board and totally reinvented Flight

Deck. The result was Super Flight Deck. This time around they painted the aircraft a bright yellow colour, so it looked less like an F4 Phantom and more like a 4p Banana. Presumably this bright hue was used in an effort to make the aircraft easier to see when it was whizzing across the living room, helping to cut down on the number of granny casualties.

The Flying Pickets — Pop Group popular around 1983

Only in a decade as musically noxious as the 1980s could a band like The Flying Pickets exist. They were an "a cappella" group, which means they used their voices in place of instruments. Or to put it another way, they were a bunch of gormless gits who stood around humming.

It worked something like this: One guy stood at the back chanting "bom-bom" in a low tone (he was the bass). Another syncopated "poms" in between the boms. Someone else went "ba-da" in a higher voice. Someone went "Da-dum." Then several people stood at the front going "Boooo!" They were the audience.

The group's big hit was a cover of Yazoo's "Only You", which secured the coveted Christmas number one spot in 1983, instantly spoiling the festive period for many of us. It was worse for people working in record shops around the country, as they had to put up with a non-stop stream of customers coming in and asking:

"Have you got that song that goes: Bada-bad-da, bada-bad-da…"

"Yes, it's-"

"Bada-bad-da, bada-bad-da, bada-bad-da…"

"'Only You' by The Flying Pickets."

"Bada-bad-da, bada-bad-da… And all I ever knew… Only you."

"There you go, that's just what it's called."

"What? Bada-bad-da?"

"Yes."

How lead singer Brian Hibbard managed to keep a straight face while singing the words over the top of all that bada-bad-dahing, Lord only knows. I suspect his large mutton-chop sideburns helped in some way – he probably grew them just to weigh his face down and prevent him from being able to laugh or smile.

The Flying Pickets had a top ten follow-up with "When You're Young and in Love", but thankfully that was the last time they bothered the charts. We'll always remember them, though, as the band who hummed so much they stank.

Ford Capri

In its advertising, Ford claimed the Capri was the car you'd promised yourself. And it was. It was the car you promised yourself you'd never buy, never drive and never travel in as a passenger.

The Capri was naffness personified. Fluffy dice and a windscreen banner with the name of you and your partner positioned just above your respective seats weren't merely optional extras. They were components as essential as the engine or steering wheel. The vehicle probably didn't start without them in place.

The coupe had a long bonnet, which meant if you were involved in a head-on smash you had plenty of time to get out of the car before you even reached the accident, and a speedometer which guessed how fast you were going rather than actually knowing. The dashboard was genuine plastic walnut and filled with clocks and dials all set in holes of varying sizes. As your Capri got older, its body would also gain holes of varying sizes, except these would be rusty ones.

The vehicle underwent various revisions during the 1970s but it was probably the Mark 3 which people remember best. This was the model driven by Bodie and Doyle in *The Professionals*. A good choice as you'd need to be a professional idiot to drive one. In later years it also starred in *Only Fools and Horses* where, as Del Boy's new vehicle, it managed the unthinkable, making his yellow Reliant Regal look classy.

It should really be driven down litter-strewn alleyways.

Frankie Goes to Hollywood — Pop Group popular around 1984–86

Frankie were all about controversy. They were about sexuality (some of the band were gay). But most of all, they were about T-shirts. Everywhere you looked in the mid-1980s, you could see a "Frankie Say" slogan shirt. Frankie sure said lots of things. He said "Relax." He said "Arm the Unemployed." He said "War, Hide Yourself."

Frankie probably did so much saying because the band sure as hell couldn't manage singing, or playing their bastard instruments for that matter. One of the band could definitely play though. Backing vocalist Paul Rutherford's tambourine solos were amazing. Rattle-rattle-rattle…

Despite being blatantly talentless Liverpudlians, Frankie had some massive hits with songs about sex ("Relax") and war ("Two Tribes"). Frankie's success was mainly the fault of the BBC and chief idiot DJ Mike Read, who instigated an unofficial ban on "Relax" due to its suggestive lyrics. This immediately ensured it would be bought by kids everywhere, who would listen to it and then ask their parents embarrassing questions about what "come" was.

The videos for these singles matched the lyrics for controversy. The original (banned) "Relax" video featured some sort of sado-masochistic orgy, with lead singer Holly Johnson being spun around on a wheel while a fat bloke ejaculated on him from a great height at the song's crescendo. Okay, so I'm lying, that would have been ridiculous. The fat chap just had a piss on him.

"Two Tribes" showed the US and Soviet presidents trying to pull each other's hair out, grab each other's knackers, kick each other up the arse and just generally put the mace into Cold War diplomacy. By the end of it all, both leaders looked like George W Bush after a pretzel eating contest.

The band's first album, *Welcome to the Pleasure Dome*, contained all their hits alongside a load of crap filler tracks (including bizarre covers of Bruce Springsteen and Burt Bacharach songs). The follow-up, *Liverpool*, skipped the hits theme and went down the 100% crap route. With no controversy to push sales it sank like a ferry failing to cross the Mersey, and the band split up shortly afterwards. Frankie say bugger. We say thank fuck.

Free School Milk — Dairy Freebies popular around 1930–80

Just the other day, I heard someone imploring "Oh why, oh why won't the government bring back school milk for our kids?" God, I hate imploring. Now exploring, that's fine, it gets people out and about and occasionally discovers a tribe deep in a forest who've managed to invent something cool like plates in their lips. They sure beat our Western TV dinner trays when it comes to mealtime convenience. But imploring is basically just whining.

School milk was a shit idea anyway. It was invariably warm and curdled, as the teacher – seemingly on purpose – always left the crates near a window in the sun, or next to a radiator in winter. So it tasted like tepid, sour crap, and the whole experience of drinking it consisted of trying to find creative ways to accidentally spill the majority of the stuff into the nearest plant pot, or perhaps into Timmy Houghton's shorts so you could point and laugh at him for wetting himself. Again.

The whole free milk scheme was just another torture in the school curriculum. As if kids didn't have enough of those already, what with sadistic PE teachers making them do sports in the pissing rain, getting regularly stabbed in the leg by compasses, and being forced to sing "Kum-Ba-Yah My Lord" on a weekly basis in assembly. It seems to me that the real reason people moan about the banishment of school milk is that Maggie "Milk Snatcher" Thatcher was behind its demise in the 1970s, and any idea of hers must be bad. Though you can hardly compare stopping milk deliveries with sinking the Belgrano or the poll tax.

The Generation Game — TV Programme popular around 1971–95

Ostensibly *The Generation Game*, originally presided over by Bruce Forsyth, was so called because it starred four teams comprising of two family members from a different generation. I reckon the real reason was because you aged 30 years in the space of the hour spent watching the show.

The idea, like the average contestant, was simple. The teams would compete against each other, starting in the first round by attempting to copy something they'd just watched an expert do. This might include throwing a vase on a potter's wheel, spinning plates, or performing open heart surgery.

The expert would then mark their efforts, usually awarding ludicrously high points to someone who'd performed atrociously. It didn't matter if their attempt at a pot looked more like a giant turd, that all the plates had broken on the first revolution, or that the patient had bled to death, so long as they'd done their best.

There would then be a play or some similar nonsense that required the

55

contestants to wear silly costumes and fall over a lot, before the not-so-grand finale: the infamous conveyor belt. This involved a load of stuff rolling past a member of the triumphant team at a fair old lick, and they won anything they could remember afterwards. There was invariably a Teasmade, a cuddly toy, a fondue set, and lots of other tat. It was like a bad jumble sale on speed.

However, it wasn't actually the games or prizes that mattered in *The Generation Game*. It was really all about the catchphrases. Bruce yammered all his classics out, from "Nice to see you, to see you, nice!" through to "Good game, good game" and not forgetting "Didn't they do well?" One of the more enigmatic offerings was the line he used to introduce the contestants: "Let's meet the eight who are going to generate!" Generate what exactly? A shit lump of clay?

After Bruce had left, Larry Grayson carried on the catchphrase mania, but with a much more camp vein. His favourites were "Oh, what a gay day!" alongside numerous stories about Everard, Slack Alice and Pop-it-in Pete, the postman. He also said "Shut that door" quite a lot, presumably referring to the exits at the back of the studio through which the audience were trying to escape in their droves.

The Generation Game went off the air in the early 1980s after viewing figures dwindled, although it was resurrected at the turn of the 1990s. There was no real attempt to alter the format, the only obvious innovation being a new host in the form of Jim Davidson. Surprisingly, as it turned out, he was to be my favourite of the three presenters. Not because he was any good of course, but because he succeeded in killing the show off permanently.

If they'd truly wanted the revived programme to succeed, the producers really should have put some effort into spicing it up a bit more. The contemporary version of Star Trek was massively popular around this time, so one possibility would have been a futuristic space-themed version called *The Next Generation Game*. New rounds could have seen contestants baking their own Cornish pasty foreheads before engaging in a battle to the death with a Klingon warrior. They might end up being decapitated by a Bat'leth blade, but at least they wouldn't be going home with a sodding fondue set.

Gobstoppers
Sweet popular around 1965–85

Parents are rarely consistent when it comes to telling their children what they can and can't do. For example, as a child you'd be regularly warned against eating too many sweets in case you ruined your appetite. Yet your parents would be more than happy for you to fill your mouth at almost any time of the day with that goliath of sweets, the jumbo gobstopper. In fact, they'd cheerfully buy you one without you even needing to nag them for it.

Looking back it's easy to see the reason for their embrace of this particular piece of hard candy. It did exactly what it claimed to do – stopped your gob from speaking. When you announced you were bored during the school holidays, a giant gobstopper would soon appear for you to suck on, and wise dads would take some on a long car journey just to prevent you from being able to ask if you were there yet. By the time you could speak, a journey from Lands End to John O'Groats could have been peacefully completed. Some gobstoppers even included bubblegum centres so when you did finish the sweet, you still couldn't speak because your jaw ended up being gummed together. Gobstoppers were massive and filled your mouth. You couldn't crunch or chew them, because they were just too solid – which is why the Americans called them jawbreakers.

However, the gobstopper was more than just a large rounded lump of sugar. It was multicoloured. As time passed and your sucking dissolved a layer of the sweet, it would change colour. You had to remove it to see what colour it was, although that gave you a chance to gulp a breath of fresh air and ask your mates what bright shade the inside of your mouth had turned.

You can still buy gobstoppers, but they aren't as popular or as large these days, mainly because they are unquestionably a choking hazard. Henry Heimlich introduced the world to his famous manoeuvre in 1974, just as gobstoppers were at the peak of their popularity. It doesn't take a genius to make the connection there.

Gonks — Toy popular around 1980–85

What was the key to passing exams? Intelligence? Hard work? Good eyesight and an exam hall seat next to the school swot? Nah. Exams, in the end, were all about gonks. The gonk was supposed to bring you luck and help you pass. It was essentially a crap teddy bear – a miniature version with no arms or legs, just a tiny pair of eyes stuck on a fluffy spherical body. The more you had, the luckier you'd be went the theory.

Gathered in a small crowd on your desk, they looked like a load of fuzzy bollocks, which, coincidentally, if you put your faith in gonks as opposed to revision, was likely to be the contents of your exam paper as well.

Grease

"So… that brings us on to Grease, the musical set in a high school in the 1950s. How's the casting going Geoff?"

"Fabulous. We've got all the main parts filled now."

"Great, so who'll be playing the young lead, Danny Zuko?"

"John Travolta."

"John Travolta? But he's–"

"Fabulous."

"Well, yes, maybe but… how old is he?"

"Twenty-three."

"Twenty-three?"

"Yes."

"Riiight. And who have you got to play the teenage Sandy?"

"You'll love this! Olivia Newton-John."

"I see. And she's how old?"

"Twenty-nine."

"Shit."

"And we've got a woman called Stockard Channing to play Rizzo."

"A woman?"

"Yes."

"Not a girl?"

"Well, I meant 'girl' of course."

"And how young is she?"

"Thirty-four."

"For fuck's sake, Geoff. What do you think the leaving age was in a typical high school in the 1950s? Who've you got to play Frenchy, your flaming mum?"

"No. She's away for two weeks in Albuquerque when we're shooting."

"Thank fu–" "But my gran is free…"

Green Shield Stamps

In the 1960s and 1970s, collecting Green Shield Stamps was a way of life. They were a bit like Panini football stickers, but for adults. Except that they didn't have footballers printed on them (they had green shields, surprisingly enough). So there was no need to swap them as they all looked the same, and collecting them was, in theory at least, actually worth doing.

Loads of shops and most supermarkets and petrol stations signed up to the scheme and gave away stamps with every purchase. The more money you spent, the more stamps you got. The idea was you'd collect as many stamps as you could, stick them in a special book and eventually, when you'd got enough, trade them in for one of the fantastic items available in the catalogue. Which actually contained pretty much everything you could ever want in 1970s Britain, ranging from toys, bathroom scales, coasters and a fondue set, to dream items like a brand new family car. Each item was priced according to the number of completed books required.

Trading in stamps involved going to the Green Shield Stamp shop, having your books inspected and the covers torn off and then getting a ticket you could swap, along with your naked books, for what you wanted. Standing in a catalogue shop and handing over a ticket to get your item sounds like Argos, doesn't it? It should do, Argos began life as a chain of Green Shield Stamp shops, but was eventually sold as a separate venture. No figures are available on how many books of stamps were required for *that* purchase.

The problem with the whole scheme was that it took ages to stick all those stamps into the books. Parents everywhere, failing to realize that child labour had long since been abolished, coerced their offspring into doing the majority of licking and sticking. Sometimes for the promise of the stamps being turned into a toy, but generally just "because."

Lots of stamps went missing, or never made it into books. Of the books that did get finished, loads never got redeemed because it took so many completed albums to get the item you wanted. Saving for a Ford Cortina was cheaper than buying one, but you might as well have been saving for a time machine, as there was fuck all chance of you ever managing to complete the necessary 1,350 books in your lifetime.

Back in the 1960s everyone was a stamp collector.

Green Slime — Novelty popular around 1977–85

A plastic tub full of green slime was an odd purchase. The stuff was simply a gelatinous pile of green goop. It was a totally useless novelty with no discernible purpose. Except, as with most useless things, children found ways to utilize them which were guaranteed to drive adults up the wall. You could:

1. Pretend you were a ghost out of *Ghostbusters*, covering yourself with a sheet and running around the living room going "Woooooo!" Which would shortly be followed by "Ow!" when you smashed your knee into the coffee table. Then you could slime people with ectoplasm, just like in the film, rubbing the green gunk on their faces, or preferably in their hair.

2. Pick off a small chunk, put it on the end of your finger, go up to somebody and pretend to pick your nose, waving around a horrible looking giant radioactive bogey with glee before wiping it on them.

3. Make a goatee beard out of the stuff, raid your mum's make-up bag and slap on some green eyeliner, put a colander on your head and apply for a part as an extra on *Doctor Who*.

4. There was absolutely nothing else you could do with green slime except ruin carpets and soft furnishings.

The Grifter — Bicycle popular around 1976–82

In the bike era just previous to the BMX, if you didn't ride a Raleigh Chopper, then you probably had a Grifter. Both were smart-looking bikes that everyone aspired to own, but they were both about as practical as a balsawood screwdriver.

The Grifter's problem was that it had a very solidly built frame which was damn heavy – much heavier than most nine-year-old Herberts. Your first go on a Grifter generally consisted of you sitting on it then toppling over in a heap. Whoever invented the phrase "It's as easy as riding a bike" didn't attempt to learn on one of these chunky fellas.

The Grifter had several other novel features. The first was the gear shift, which was on the right hand side grip of the handlebars. To change between the three gears you twisted it, so it was like a throttle and you could pretend you were revving up just as if you were on a real motorbike – although this gave you nasty blisters on your thumb. Secondly, you could bend the front mudguard flap up so it caught on the tyre, and as you rode along it rubbed on the chunky tyre grip and made a noise that sounded like a motorcycle (eventually it burnt a hole in your mudguard, and your dad got very cross indeed.)

The Grifter was a motorbike minus the motor just as the Chopper was designed after the customized Harley–Davidsons of the same name, making both bikes ideal for any would-be Evel Knievels. Just like their hero, kids could set up jumps and fail miserably to clear them. It was impossible to leap over a row of Double Deckers on the great lump of metal that was the Grifter, anyway. And we're talking the chocolate bars, not the buses.

Head Bags — School Bag popular around 1985–95

Why was a school bag with "Head" written on the side of it popular? Something like "Puma" you could understand – a sports bag with a powerful, lightning quick animal on it. But what the hell did Head mean? It made no sense. And if it did make any sense, it was probably rude sense, and not the sort of thing a schoolboy should have plastered across his holdall. Also, where were the Shoulders, Knees and Toes bags, to fill out the range?

No one with any real nouse owned a Head bag, and not just because of the incomprehensibly crap brand name. There was also the fact that if it was left lying around the form room unattended, it was inevitable that the class wag would Tippex on the "Dick" prefix the owner rightly deserved.

He-Man — Cartoon popular around 1983–85

If you were to imagine a being worthy of the title "Master of the Universe", your mind's eye would likely conjure a potent image. Perhaps an enigmatic, towering figure, with a cowl pulled over his head, and two piercing specks of light for eyes that gleamed in the inky blackness of his hood, like singularities spiralling into infinity.

Whatever personification of power you might choose, it most definitely wouldn't be a fake-tanned speedo-clad twat with a blond bob haircut and oiled nipples. He-Man, for all the bluster of his name, was about as macho as a rose and apricot face mask. This didn't matter to kids in the 1980s, of course, and come break-time the playground was full of tykes waving around imaginary Swords of Greyskull, fighting all the unfortunate skinny kids who were arbitrarily declared Skeletors.

The cartoon itself was unbelievably corny and repetitive, with every episode following pretty much the same template. Pink blouse-wearing Prince Adam would hold his sword aloft, shout "I have the power!" and then turn into He-Man. Surprisingly, his mission wasn't to find the nearest disco playing thumping loud euro-pop; instead, he had to confront Skeletor over his latest evil scheme.

Battle-Cat, also known as Cringer. Not surprising given the prat on his back.

Skeletor would then fight dirty, He-Man would refuse to stoop to his level, and our homoerotic hero would win. To close the show, the producers would wheel out a moral, some of which were sensible lessons such as: "Don't disrespect your parents, kids." The writers soon ran out of decent ideas though, and the morals became banal, irrelevant or just plain stupid. "Don't hit your grandma over the head with an umbrella, kids." The cartoon only ever existed to entice gullible children to buy action figures of He-Man and Skeletor, not to mention their miscellaneous cohorts. Richer children could afford the Castle Greyskull replica, where their plastic He-Man could hang out with fellow do-good'ers Ram-Man and Fisto in the dungeon, and parents could wonder what the hell was going on in the cartoon designers' heads.

Hi-de-Hi!   TV Programme popular around 1980–88

Every morning, Gladys Pugh would greet guests staying at the holiday camp in this BBC sitcom with a cheery "Hi-de-Hi!" over the tannoy, complete with an annoying three-note musical accompaniment. And all the Maplins campers would shout back a dour "Ho-de-Ho!" in unison. Not like in the real world where they'd have told her exactly where to stick her xylophone first thing in the bloody morning.

Hi-de-Hi's cast of yellow-coats were a diverse bunch with a complex map of relationships. Gladys fancied Jeffrey the camp manager, the stuck-up married dance instructors didn't fancy each other, and the cantankerous alcoholic Punch-and-Judy man fancied punching the kids in the face. There was also Ted, the camp comic, and his hapless assistant Spike. The latter would invariably get dressed up in a novelty costume and then be pushed into the swimming pool in every episode. How we laughed – it was pure comedy bronze.

The underdog in all this was Peggy the chalet maid (played by Su Pollard). She was a hyperactive cleaner who desperately wanted to be a yellow-coat, although to be honest the bespectacled gawp was more in need of a white coat, one of the ones with arms that fasten up

Gladys was the proud owner of the world's smallest xylophone.

nice and tightly. As mad as a brush, Peggy was never to be seen without her dirty mop. That bird's nest of lankly permed blonde hair was a real state, to be sure.

While her character never won any of Maplins' poolside beauty contests (obviously), Su was inexplicably awarded the coveted "Rear of the Year" accolade in 1988. How on Earth she came to be shortlisted in the first place is a mystery, but you'd have to assume the judges overheard someone talking about "that great arse" on *Hi-de-Hi* and got the wrong end of the stick.

The Incredible Hulk — TV Programme popular around 1978–82

When the subject of this TV show comes up in conversation (which, granted, isn't very often) there's one question that always arises. Surprisingly it isn't "How did that load of crap ever get made?" but it's actually "How come when David Banner changes into the Hulk, his shirt splits and he tears it off, but his trousers remain resolutely undamaged?" The answer, of course, is it was a family TV programme and no one wanted to see a giant green cock on screen. Let alone one with its knob out.

The show was based on the popular Marvel comic, but various changes were made for no apparent reason. In the comics the Hulk's alter ego is Doctor Bruce Banner. In the TV show, he's Doctor David Banner. The rumour was the switch was made because "Bruce" was seen to be a bit of a gay name – worrying news for millions of macho Australians – although it's more likely TV execs simply felt "Bill

Bixby is Bruce Banner" was too much of a tongue twister.

Changing the name of the miserable green giant to The Mediocre Hulk would have been a smarter move, because that's exactly what he was in this show. The comic book version could lift mountains, hurl tractors into outer space and jump over skyscrapers. The TV one – played by bodybuilder Lou Ferrigno – could barely manage to push over a badly mortared brick wall or roll a car off a cliff (certainly not if it had its handbrake on). And worst of all, whenever the Hulk was filmed running through the streets it was clear to anyone watching that he had green slippers on his feet. Maybe the gay thing wasn't so far from the truth.

Every episode involved David Banner wandering from town to town, looking for a cure for his condition (a bottle of Hulk-No-More possibly, or Green-Be-Gone). He was pursued by a reporter called Mr McGee, and invariably got himself into some sort of scrape whereby he became angry or upset and changed into the Hulk. A complex process which involved him shouting "Noooooooooo!" and popping in some white contact lenses.

Then the fat bodybuilder in green paint and a fright-wig would turn up in clothes two sizes too small, tear them off, and roar. It was far from cutting-edge effects, even back then. The whole scene probably cost a tenner to make. I'm surprised they didn't spray-paint one half of Lou and film him from that angle in every shot. Or better yet just dub some old footage of Kermit waving his arms. It would have been just as convincing.

At the start of every programme, they'd show a scene in which David Banner would warn Mr McGee: "Don't make me angry. You wouldn't like me when I'm angry." Which was slightly redundant as no-one liked him anyway. If you were having a party you'd rather invite the Hulk. He might smash the place up and scare the shit out of all your guests, but at least he wouldn't bore them to tears.

The Incredible Hulk. And his incredibly silky indestructible boxers.

I-Spy

These little books sold to kids by the bucket-full in their heyday. There was a whole range of them: *I-Spy in the Garden, I-Spy in the Town, I-Spy Cars, I-Spy Pub Signs...* The idea was that when you spotted something related to the subject, you'd tick it off in your book. Then you'd... well, that was it, really.

When you'd ticked off everything listed in the book, and ticked off your parents by continually pointing out objects – "I-Spy an oak tree!"; "I-Spy a blackbird!"; "I-Spy a used prophylactic!" – you could send it off to Big Chief I-Spy at the publishers. Big Chief Cash-Cow – sorry, I-Spy – would then send you back a certificate of achievement and a genuine Injun' feather (freshly plucked from his pigeon loft that very morning).

The whole Red Indian mythos that surrounded the I-Spy series was a bit of an enigma. The company even had the address of their headquarters down as The-Wigwam-by-the-Green, London, even though the "wigwam" (actually in Paddington) was in fact a smoke-stained office above a hardware store, probably with a battered old tomahawk and a stuffed alligator hung on the walls. However, come the 1980s and the advent of political correctness, they started to get into big heap trouble for all the Indian references, so had to drop them.

This meant no more dressing up in Red Indian costumes for the employees, who were forced to install a fax machine to use instead of smoke-signals when communicating with the Big Chief. They were also made to sign a truce with the cowboys from up the road (the BT office in North Paddington).

Izal

The school toilets of old were a place of fear. And not just because you ran the risk of being bullied by the hard fifth-formers who hung out there, smoking and making up stories about who they'd shagged.

Having your abusive peers flush your head down the toilet just after Fatty Patterson had peppered the basin was nothing compared to the horror you experienced if you suddenly found yourself in need of a dump while on school property. The problem wasn't the actual act of defecating, it was the aftermath. The moment when you stood up, pants around your ankles, and tried to wipe your bum with medicated Izal.

These days, toilet paper is soft, quilted and luxurious. Izal was hard, shiny and brutal. It was basically like a sheet of greaseproof tracing paper – except it was shit-proof as well. Instead of cleaning your arse, it merely spread everything around. The result was a crap stained crack with more Klingons than your average *Star Trek* movie. Some versions of Izal had "Now wash your hands" printed on each sheet. "Now wash your arse" would've been a lot more appropriate.

On top of that, Izal had almost lethally sharp edges, so one careless wipe could inflict serious damage. If they'd made the Andrex adverts with Izal, the paper-entwined Labrador pup would've rolled playfully down the stairs, and left a trail of freshly amputated limbs behind it.

God knows why schools insisted on stocking the stuff. There might as well have been a roll of barbed wire in every cubicle. The pre-toilet paper concept of having squares of neatly cut up newspaper in the khazi would have provided a far softer and more absorbent alternative. Not only that, but after a good wipe you'd have truthfully been able to say that *The Sun* shone out of your arse…

Jubbly

Lolly popular around 1960–80

Jubblies were incredibly unwieldy and unimaginative ice lollies. These "frozen drinks" (as they were officially known) were simply huge triangular lumps of flavoured ice. You could get them in several different flavours, although the shops only ever seemed to stock orange, orange, and for a bit of extra variety, orange. As far as Jubblies were concerned, oranges really were the only fruit.

You consumed a Jubbly by sucking on it until all the flavoured juice had been tapped, leaving you with a completely inedible chunk of ice the size of a small glacier. Very useful. This was generally disposed of in some nefarious manner, such as lobbing it at a cat, or putting it down the back of the shirt of someone you didn't like (or secretly fancied).

Despite these issues, some powerful people tried Jubblies. Remember the Queen famously had one in the 1970s? It was all over the papers. No, wait a minute; that was a Jubilee, wasn't it? My mistake.

The innocent times of these icebergs are now gone, and these days, if you're down the park on a hot summer's day and you lean across for a suck on your girlfriend's Jubbly, you'll probably find that (a) it isn't orange flavoured and (b) she'll either slap you hard across the face, or you'll both end up getting arrested.

Junior Chemistry Set — Educational Toy popular around 1965–85

These sets came in hefty great boxes and generally consisted of a small and rubbish microscope, a pair of tweezers, some spatulas, pipettes and experiment dishes. The main ingredient was the 20 stoppered test tubes full of chemicals, of which 10 were seriously poisonous if ingested, 6 could be mixed together to create home-made explosives, and the remaining 4 turned your brother's hair into a rainbow of diverse and amazingly bright colours when you put them in his shampoo.

This was the Christmas present every loathing parent gave their unwanted nine-year-old offspring. It was the gift that said: "We made a mistake by not going down the clinic a decade ago." If you didn't hospitalize yourself in the first three months of owning the set, your folks got their money back.

Quite how the Junior Chemistry Set got off the drawing board and into production, when other perfectly good ideas such as the Junior Fire-Eating Set, the Junior Cannabis Farm and the Junior Bomb Disposal Kit all remained unrealized, we'll just never know.

Kaliber — Drink popular around 1985–90

Back in the 1980s, Billy Connolly popped up on our TV screens in adverts which tried to convince us to drink beer. Not any old beer mind you, this was a new beverage from Guinness called Kaliber, an alcohol-free lager. Which is quite possibly the stupidest invention ever – it was quite appropriate that they hired a comedian to promote it, as it was a fucking joke.

Okay, so the idea was you could go out and enjoy a drink without getting pissed and being unable to drive home. The problem is you might drink, say, a glass of low alcohol wine in order to savour it without getting bladdered, but nobody, repeat nobody, drinks lager to enjoy the flavour. The main reason you guzzle the golden loopy juice is because you want to get wasted, go for a kebab and then have a fight over a taxi. Let's face it, alcohol-free lager is as bloody pointless as a sex-free brothel, or oxygen-free air. And given the choice of the latter or an evening spent drinking Kaliber, I'd go for the lung-fulls of nitrogen and carbon dioxide every time. At least there'd be no going to the toilets every ten minutes.

In truth, the beer wasn't totally alcohol free – it did contain a tiny amount. This meant if you somehow managed to down 50-odd pints of the stuff you might start to get a touch merry and tell your mates what great and sterling pals they were. Although if they'd been buying you Kaliber all night, clearly that wasn't the case.

Ketchips — Food popular around 1988–92

Take Britain's favourite food – chips – and inject them with Britain's favourite sauce – ketchup – and what have you got? I've no idea, but it certainly isn't Ketchips. These were soggy mush-flavoured potato croquettes filled with a lava-temperature vinegar paste. Served up on a plate and haemorrhaging crimson they looked for all the world like oven-cooked used tampons. Yum.

Kia-Ora — Drink popular around 1960–85

You can still buy Kia-Ora today, but it's nowhere near as popular as it was in the 1970s and 1980s. At that time, it was pretty much the only drink you could purchase in a cinema – it came in a clear plastic carton and the juice was such a luminous orange colour it doubled as a handy lamp, helping you to locate your seat in the darkness.

The thing most people remember about Kia-Ora is the advert in which a young black chap is pursued by a group of crows who all want some of his orange juice drink. He won't share it because it's too orangey for them – apparently it's just for him and his dog. So the crows offer to be his dog and start barking. Then one of the crows grabs the sun from the sky and starts playing basketball with it, before bouncing it onto the head of a big fat mama where it turns into a bag of washing – which then spills out and starts dancing before becoming a wet suit for a crow following behind.

All of which suggests it wasn't just crows the E-number filled juice was too "orangey" for.

Kim Wilde

Pop Star popular around 1981–88

There are lies, damned lies, and statistics… followed by damned statistics, and finally, Prime Minister's question time. The whole history of humankind has pretty much been a tissue of lies all round, and Kim Wilde joined in with a good old blow on the fibbing hanky in 1981 when she released her debut hit, "Kids in America". It might not have been on a par with WMDs in Iraq but the song was packed with more porkies than a pig farming convention.

"We're the kids in America," Kim claimed, although she was 21 at the time the record was released, so hardly a kid. Also, she was born in Chiswick, lived in Hertfordshire and went to college in St Albans. All of which, last time I checked, are in England, not America. Still, I guess a more truthful version wouldn't have had quite the same appeal:

> "We're the adults of Ware, Hertfordshire (whoa-ho!)
> We're the adults of Ware, Hertfordshire (whoa-ho!)
> Everybody lives for the Poles Lane Litter-Pick.
> La, la, la-la, la la.
> La, la, la-la, la laaa.
> Hey!"

Even though it was a total fabrication, "Kids in America" launched Kim's career and she went on to have a number of hits with various bland pop tunes such as "Cambodia", "You Keep Me Hangin' On", and "Four Letter Word" (I'm guessing the word in question was "shit" because the song certainly was).

Eventually, she fell from public favour and was forced to reinvent herself as a celebrity gardener. She's since written several books on the subject including *Gardening with Children,* which seems like an odd idea to me. I usually find gardening with a trowel delivers better results.

Kipper Tie — Fashion Accessory popular around 1967–80

The kipper was the tie equivalent of flared trousers. It was a thick swathe of material which got so wide towards the bottom, it wasn't far off becoming a waistcoat, albeit one you knotted around your neck.

The proper attire for an interview at the Open University.

But despite its ludicrous appearance and impracticality – if a sudden gust of wind whipped this monstrosity behind your neck, you'd be looking at possible whiplash injuries – some people just loved to stand out from the crowd by wearing one. And the crowd just loved to stand out from the wearer, preferably at least a mile away from them, three miles if they were the zany type of fashion victim who preferred a brightly coloured purple or psychedelic green kipper.

It isn't right to refer to the wearers of the kipper tie as fashion victims though. They were surely criminals who deserved to be arrested by the fashion police, then tried and sentenced. To death, naturally.

They'd be well equipped to deal with that prospect, mind you. Their kipper could double as a tablecloth for their last meal, and it would make a sturdy length of material to hang them from.

Knight Rider — TV Programme popular around 1983–86

Before David Hasselhoff starred in *Baywatch* – playing the one tit on the show that nobody wanted to watch, in slow-motion or otherwise – he was best known for his role as Michael Knight, a "Young loner on a crusade to champion the cause of the innocent, the helpless, the powerless, in a world of criminals who operate above the law." Seeing as they were in the criminal underworld, you'd have thought they'd have operated under the law, if anywhere.

The show was conceived as a kind of Western for modern times, with the lone ranger Knight riding his trusty horse-powered steed; a car called KITT. This vehicle – Knight Industries Two Thousand – was a pretty impressive piece of machinery. It was an artificially intelligent black Pontiac Firebird Trans Am that could drive itself, was bullet-proof and had an incredibly powerful engine. It was also camper than a campervan, with a voice more to John Inman than John Wayne.

KITT was one of the two main reasons to watch *Knight Rider*. The other one being there was nothing else on and you couldn't find the remote. How we marvelled at a car that could drive itself. And wasn't Herbie. How we gasped in amazement at the programme's incredible effects. Or rather didn't. To simulate the Pontiac doing several hundred miles-per-hour the director simply speeded the film up, so much so that you'd momentarily check under your backside to see if you'd accidentally sat on the video remote and hit the fast forward button. It was that bad, if you flicked over and hadn't seen the show before, you'd be forgiven for thinking that Benny Hill had treated himself to a shiny new black sports car. All that was missing was the music.

The other impressive piece of effects wizardry was KITT's turbo boost. This was a button which Michael could press when he'd got himself into a ridiculous predicament, such as being out-acted by a talking car – I mean, such as driving straight towards a juggernaut at high speed. The turbo boost would rocket the car into the air and over any obstacle like magic. It was magic, because when the camera angle switched for

the landing scene, the Pontiac went from coming in at a near perpendicular total write-off angle to a mysteriously smooth touchdown. The Trans Am's tyres might have been slick, but the directing wasn't.

Never mind the woeful effects, acting, scripts, plots and all the other little niggles. *Knight Rider* still had that one admirable feature – the car. KITT looked damn impressive, particularly with

If pictures could paint words, this one would simply say: 'Mid-life Crisis'.

that strobing red light on the bonnet. Although for the ultimate in cool, it really should have had the Firebird transfer on the hood. God, so they say, is in the decals.

The Krankies — Double Act popular around 1979–86

Knock down the Krankies with a football and win a prize. Not to mention the gratitude of the nation.

To many men, the idea of their girlfriend or wife dressing up in a school uniform is the ultimate sexual thrill. So it's hard to imagine the disappointment that Ian Tough must have felt when his wife Janette offered to slip on her uniform and came back into the bedroom… dressed as a schoolboy. And worse still, insisting that Ian call her Wee Jimmy Krankie from now on, and pretend to be her father. Poor bastard. I suppose that's what you call tough luck.

The duo took their odd brand of entertainment on the road and went on to have a successful and frankly awful showbiz career, appearing on *Crackerjack* before hosting their own TV shows like *Krankie Klub* and *Krankies Electronic Komik*. At four foot five, Janette was as short in stature as she was in talent, and anyone who still thinks sarcasm is the lowest form of wit never saw her attempts at comedy on those programmes. The Krankies' act was cheesier than a quattro formaggio pizza, and their catchphrase – "Fan-Dabi-Dozi" – was just horrible.

All that said, later on in their career they did reach considerable heights. Or at least Janette did, when they moved into panto and she found herself perched at the top of a beanstalk. Briefly. But then she came over all Fan-Dabi-Dizzy and plummeted downwards. The audience, understandably, was shocked, stunned and appalled. As anyone would be, having paid good money to see the Krankies. Some folks were quite surprised by the accident, too. If Ian was left wondering what had happened to his wife – at the top of the beanstalk one minute, gone the next – a unified shout of "she's beneath you!" would have helped. The seasoned panto performer has doubtless heard phrases like that a lot in the past. Mostly from his family and friends.

Leg Warmers   Fashion Accessory popular around 1980–89

Leg warmers started life as something dancers wore but thanks to films such as *Fame* and *Flashdance* they quickly became a mainstream fashion. This was despite the fact that they were nothing more impressive than a pair of baggy knee-length socks with the feet cut off.

The purpose of leg warmers is, ostensibly at least, to warm the lower legs. But is that really somewhere you ever get cold? When the temperature drops you feel it in your extremities – your fingers, toes, ears or nose. Have you ever heard of a polar

She's got leg warmers... She knows how to use them.

explorer returning from a sub-zero expedition with frostbitten shins? If there's one thing you can guarantee not to find in an Arctic adventurer's survival kit, it's leg warmers (and fingerless gloves).

But although they didn't actually serve any useful warming purpose, leg warmers still found a willing target audience. For girls with outlandishly large calves that tapered into freakishly thin ankles, they were a dream come true.

Lightsaber
Toy popular around 1977–85

Back in 1977, everyone wanted a lightsaber, thanks to the black crash-helmet wearing sociopath we'd seen waving his red one around in *Star Wars*. The toy versions of this deadly energy weapon were extremely popular with kids, who were desperate to get hold of what was essentially a coloured plastic tube with a small bulb in it. Or to put it another way, a torch.

Now I don't know if you've ever taken a torch and whacked it into a dining room table, a couple of doors, a kitchen work-top, the washing machine, the dog and several of your mates. But torch bulbs are rather fragile things, and the light bit of the lightsaber had around the same life expectancy as a Terry's Chocolate Orange in the vicinity of Dawn French.

And even if your lightsaber didn't break, you could guarantee that one other obvious problem would rear its ugly head. Imagine if *Star Wars* had been like this:

"Luke, close your eyes, use the force with your lightsaber, be at one with it."

"But Obi-Wan, its batteries have run out!"

"You don't need them, Luke. Just use the power of your mind. Do you think that Darth Vader has need of batteries?"

"Yeah he does. His dad bought him a set of Lithium rechargeables for Christmas. And what did my step-dad get me? A gay robot and a mobile dustbin. Hrrmph."

"You have much to learn about the ways of the universe, young Skywalker."

"Bugger this, I'm off down the all-night garage for some Duracell…"

Liquorice Root
Sweet popular around 1930–85

Some people like liquorice, other people hate it. But even those who love the black stuff need convincing to try the root variety, which is essentially just a twig you chew on. Sure, it has an undeniably liquorice taste, but it's difficult to overcome the fact that getting to that flavour involves sucking on a dirty piece of wood.

The root was popular during the war, when it was one of the few sweets that wasn't rationed – in fact it was probably one of the few sweets they had a surplus of. It was still available to buy in rubbish sweet shops in the 1980s for some reason. They were probably still flogging off their stock from the forties.

Liquorice root wasn't really something kids bought themselves, except as a one-off for shock novelty value ("Look! I'm eating a stick!"). Instead parents would buy it for their offspring either because they viewed it as a healthy sugar-free treat that wouldn't spoil the appetite, or because they'd eaten it growing up and wanted to share the experience. You didn't bite bits off and swallow them, and there was no danger of getting a splinter in your tongue. You just kept sucking and chewing on the fibres until they lost their taste.

Liquorice root was certainly an intriguing piece of confectionery that never failed to pique a child's curiosity. Upon being given a bag of it, you wanted to know how bits of wood could taste of liquorice, you wanted to know where they came from, and how they were prepared. Mostly though, you just wanted to know why your parents hated you so much they'd given you this crap to chomp on instead of buying you some proper sweets.

London to Brighton in Three-and-a-Half Minutes
TV Interlude popular around 1983–84

In the early days of TV, when most programmes were live, things often didn't run quite as smoothly as they should have. Occasionally a show would finish prematurely, leaving a bit of a gap to fill. In 1952, someone at the BBC came up with the idea of filling it with a train journey. It's safe to assume that particular someone was quite a boring person. Although I suppose it's possible the idea was simply born from a leap of lateral thinking – "Got to fill a gap… a gap… mind the gap… trains!"

Obviously a real train journey would have been a bit, well, long. So they used "trick photography" to speed things up. *London to Brighton in Four Minutes* was exactly that. Four minutes of watching a train go from one station to the next. It was boring as hell.

And then in 1983, when they really should have known better, the BBC remade it. In colour, 30 seconds faster and with a synthesized pop tune burbling along in the background, along with some train noises thrown in for good measure. That's 30 years of progress for you.

In all seriousness, you have to wonder what the fuck they were thinking. Surely they could have come up with something more interesting? A fast-forward through the raising of the *Mary Rose*, a speeded up Rubik's Cube solution, or the best of *Cheggers Plays Pop* perhaps. Mind you, they'd have had to slow that last one down considerably if they wanted to fill an entire three-and-a-half minute timeslot.

Love Bites — Skin Blemishes popular around 1965–85

You don't really see much of love bites these days, but they were all the rage amongst youngsters in decades past. If a teenager suddenly appeared at the breakfast table wearing a polo neck jumper during the height of summer, this could mean only one thing. They had been bitten by the love bug behind the bike sheds.

A love bite was invariably placed on the neck for maximum visibility, although it didn't have to involve biting as such. A good hard suck was all that was required to bruise and mark the skin with a purple-red lip shape. Naturally, there are better places to be sucked hard than the neck, but as a teenage boy you were just happy that a girl had come within a foot of you without vomiting.

Girls got love bites from boys too, but they had to be especially careful to hide them from mum using the traditional polo neck, maybe a plaster, or as the playground rumours had it, you could rub toothpaste on them as a cure if you were really desperate. In actual fact this did fuck all, except possibly polish your boyfriend's teeth up the next time he did his Dracula impression.

While love bites might have been hidden away at home, they were proudly displayed as a badge of honour at school. If you had one, you were cool. If you had two or three, you were really cool. More than this, however, and you started to look like a half-munched extra who'd escaped from *Night of the Living Dead*.

It was all too tempting as a spotty virginal Herbert of a lad to take matters into your own hands – as if they weren't overworked enough – and if a girl wouldn't pay you any attention, give yourself some love bites with the help of a vacuum cleaner hose. The problem was these could look a bit too perfectly circular to be real, and besides once you'd started down that route it was only a matter of time before the Hoover hose got put to another, more deviant use.

Maggie Thatcher — Prime Minister popular around 1979–90

"Maggie Thatcher, Milk Snatcher" they called her, when she was education secretary, because she ended free school milk. It would have been "Thatch the Snatch" for short, but that sounds too much like an instruction for ladies to keep their private parts warmer. The Iron Lady ruled with an iron fist. She was the first woman PM this country had, and likely the last as long as we can remember what happened during her term of office… Three-and-a-half million unemployed. An unnecessary war with Argentina over some sheep on an island. Crushing the miners. The whole poll tax debacle. And so on. We'd have all been so much happier if she had stayed working with the vegetables in the Grantham grocery where she was born, instead of the vegetables in her cabinet.

Eventually, even her own party came to their senses and back-stabbed her, forcing her to resign in 1990. The Iron Lady was then replaced by the Grey Man. While Thatcher had undeniably curried favour with some of the electorate, Major went on to lose the Conservative majority in a spectacular defeat in 1997, because he spent too much time favouring Currie with his electorate.

Magic 8-Ball — Novelty popular around 1960–85

The decline in religion in this country can be partially blamed on the popularity of the Magic 8-Ball, which introduced kids everywhere to the joys of the occult. The oversized all-seeing, all-knowing billiard ball looked harmless enough, but it was in fact a spherical gateway to Hell. Within six months of receiving one, a previously model child would be conducting séances, performing ritual sacrifices and declaring his or her love for Satan while naked on the roof of the school gymnasium.

Odd really, when you consider an exchange with the Magic 8-Ball generally went something like this:

"Can you tell me my future oh Magic 8-Ball?"
Signs Point to Yes.
"Skill! Okay, will Cathy go out with me?"
Concentrate and Ask Again.
"I am concentrating. So will she?"
Ask Again Later.

"Fuck off, I'm asking now."

My Reply is No.

"No what? No she won't go out with me?" *Most Likely.*

"Most likely she won't go out with me?"

Better Not Tell You Now.

"What? Tell me, tell me! You know something don't you?"

Don't Count on It.

"Look, tell me if Cathy will go out with me or I'll throw you against the wall. Understand?" *Yes.*

"So will she go out with me?"

You May Rely on It.

"I may rely on it?"

Yes, Definitely.

"Excellent. Hey Cathy, want to go out with me?"

"Piss off retard. I saw you talking to yourself."

Magic Eye

Published in the 1990s, the Magic Eye series consisted of picture books filled with autostereograms. On the face of it, they were psychedelic and colourful 2D patterns, a bit like Jackson Pollock's paintings (but not worth nearly as much). However – and this was the clever bit – if you stared at them really hard for a couple of minutes, and let your eyes sort of de-focus, then stared a little longer and a little harder, you eventually got to the point where you succeeded. In giving yourself a blinding headache.

Some people claimed to be able see a 3D image materialize, almost floating off the page. The key technique was that even though you were staring, you had to look through the page and let the focus of your eyes relax, possibly to the point of going cross-eyed. Hitting yourself on the head really hard with a hammer might aid this process, but it was bound to worsen any potential headache.

After all that effort, when you did eventually glimpse something, the 3D effect was novel for about ten seconds, then you'd realize you had just spent a chunk of your life concentrating harder than your average ancient Greek philosopher in order to glimpse a vision of a badly drawn 3D elephant. Or some 3D spheres. In the end, again like Jackson's paintings, autostereograms were a load of Pollocks.

Magnum, P.I.
TV Programme popular around 1981–90

Magnum was a private dick, and a gutsy, brave one at that. Well, he had to be. Going outside wearing *those* shirts and *that* moustache took balls of steel. Come to think of it, Magnum was more of a public dick than a private one.

But being Thomas Magnum wasn't all bad. In every episode he got to burn around in a convertible Ferrari 308 GTS and loll about on a luxurious Hawaiian beachfront estate. Neither of these were actually his but in fact belonged to a mega-rich novelist who employed him as part-time security. Obviously the elite classes let any old hairy Tom dick into their manor in those days.

The Mary Rose
Historic Event popular around 1982

Every person of a certain age in the 1960s can tell you where they were the exact moment they heard Kennedy had been shot. Similarly, every child in the 1980s can recall exactly where they were the moment that a sixteenth century Tudor warship called the *Mary Rose* was raised from her resting place on the Solent seabed. Bored out of their brains in front of the school TV.

That the event was televised at all is staggering. It was hardly up there with the moon landings, after all. It was far from riveting viewing – just lots of lapping waves, winching and long lingering shots of men in waterproofs and wellies.

When the wreck finally broke the surface it was like a large-scale recreation of a champion fisherman landing an old boot. Instead of a resplendent galleon the cradle came up carrying what appeared to be a giant whale turd. We all laughed, expecting them to chuck it back into the water and try again, but instead they carefully lowered it on to a waiting tug. What? This was what we'd been waiting all those hours for? At that precise moment we knew just how the wreck's mast felt. Ripped off.

Perhaps we shouldn't have been surprised though. After 437 years under the water, the *Mary Rose* was never going to be anything other than a right load of old ship.

Milk Tray Ads
Advertisements popular around 1970–85

It's Valentine's Day. You're a really adventurous bloke who works for the secret service or something, and you're handsome and debonair, never to be seen without

79

your jewel encrusted Rolex and crisp black polo-neck ironed to within an inch of its life. Where others use the stairs, you abseil; where others catch a bus, you catch a cable car and then jump from it to ski down a mountain. You're a different class. So what do you buy your fair lady as a gift, from one supreme lover to another? A box of cheap chocolates you bought down the Shell garage. Naturally.

If these adverts lied about the bloke, they weren't any more truthful about the woman. The recipient of the daringly delivered chocolates was generally some svelte raven-haired maiden, dressed in a flimsy nightie which clung to her sensuously curved body. If she was a proper chocoholic, as the ad's slogan suggested, she'd have been a bed-ridden walrus with ankles the size of oak trees and sweat rings which were more like reservoirs.

And while it would be sad for her parents when she passed away from diabetes at the age of 40, at least they'd have a ready-made epitaph for her gravestone: "And all because the lady loved Milk Tray."

Minipops — TV Programme popular around 1983

Minipops was like an early 1980s version of *Stars in Their Eyes Kids*. Children would come out on stage, pretending to be adults, and perform their favourite pop hits. However, there were several striking differences between the two shows. There was no Cat Deeley on Minipops, the kids weren't competing with one another, and they lip-synched rather than sang. Without a doubt though, the biggest difference was in the wardrobe department. In *Stars in Their Eyes*, normal kids walk off stage and return through a cloud of smoke – authentically and somewhat cutely – dressed as the pop star they're intending to imitate. This might be a mini-Noddy Holder complete with long permed hair, comedy sideburns and platform shoes, or a mini-Cher in a long black wig. In *Minipops*, every girl on stage appeared to have been dressed to resemble Jodie Foster's child prostitute from *Taxi Driver*. They all wore very short skirts, high heels and were caked in make-up – glossy lipstick, blusher, the works.

It was creepy and disturbing television. Watching a fully made-up ten-year-old lip-synching to songs about love and other adult themes, while showing a bit of leg or flashing her knickers and prancing about in high heels was wrong on more levels than Dante himself could have imagined.

Quite who the target audience was supposed to be it's hard to guess. Although I'd imagine the letters of protest Channel 4 received when the show was cancelled

Mistletoe and Wine

Christmas time, mistletoe and wine,
A shit song that doesn't really rhyme,
Put Cliff's record on the fire, not under the tree,
A time for rejoicing as it burns brightly.

Mittens on a String

Mittens were designed as gloves for very young kids. Or idiots. And mittens on a string were essentially mittens for very young idiots. They were a pair of mittens with a string which connected them, running up through the sleeves and across your back underneath your coat, so it wasn't possible for them to get pulled off and lost.

It was pretty embarrassing to be made to wear these, even at primary school. As if the knee-length grey shorts and turd-brown sandals weren't bad enough. Worse still was when your classmates worked out that if you were scratching a spot or picking your nose, if they yanked your other arm backwards you'd smack yourself in the face.

Mittens on a string were basically devices of humiliation and torture. It was a time in which dignity meant nothing to mums. If the mothers of the UK had been kids range fashion designers, we could have experienced a whole new line of amazing convenience clothing, such as intelligent shoes which picked themselves up when you walked to prevent scuffing. Or socks which, when they fell down, pulled themselves up automatically. Over the knees. Or pants which detected soilage and… well, let's not go there.

Monkey

Monkey, the eponymous star of this surreal live-action Japanese TV series, was the king of a monkey tribe. This, you'd imagine, would mean he was a monkey. Far from it. He was supposed to be, but in reality he was just a fairly normal looking bloke with giant mutton-chop sideburns. A bit like an oriental Noddy Holder.

If it wasn't for "Monkey Magic", the programme's seriously catchy theme tune, most viewers wouldn't have had a clue what the hell it was all about. Thankfully, the song's lyrics helped to explain it perfectly:

"Born from an egg on a mountain top

Funkiest monkey that ever popped..."

On second thoughts forget that. The theme tune was, like the show, madder than a box of chimp eggs.

Monkey himself was a cheeky little chap who could muster an impressive range of hugely exaggerated expressions, ranging from open-mouthed horror through to face screwed up with disgust. These various facial emotions came in very handy, as you needed to read them when the badly dubbed dialogue – spoken in English but with dire oriental accents – didn't make any bloody sense. Which was fairly often.

The series' plot centred around a lengthy pilgrimage, and a typical episode would involve Monkey travelling somewhere with his three friends. These were Pigsy (an insatiably lecherous and moronic pig-man), Sandy (a man who was formerly a water sprite, and was just as wet in human form) and Tripitaka (a male priest). Monkey would sulk, Pigsy would try to sneak a look at Tripitaka's tits – he was played by a sexy young woman – and then they'd be attacked by a demon. I say demon, but as you'd expect from a show with no costume budget, it would just be some random bloke with his face painted red and some coloured flags tied to his arms.

Our heroes would hit the demon with an assortment of sticks and gardening implements – Pigsy used a rake – and at some point Monkey would wave his fingers in front of his mouth, whistle and summon a magical pink cloud that he could fly around on. Or possibly he just dropped some acid, I'm not sure.

Whenever Monkey was playing the fool, which was most of the time, Tripitaka could bring him back into line by doing a spot of special chanting. This would cause Monkey's enchanted golden headband (which looked suspiciously like one of Wonder Woman's cast-offs) to tighten around his cranium. He was just lucky not to have been given a golden jockstrap to wear. He'd certainly have pulled some faces when *that* sprang into action.

The show always closed with a Zen-like moral which was guaranteed to perplex Westerners and leave more questions than answers. "Give up winning and losing, then find joy." No – find a draw, surely? "Grey hairs do not make a wise man." So are pensioners wise to use Just For Men? It was all too confusing for words.

There were some pretty unfathomable hairstyles in fashion during the 1980s, but the mullet was the most inexplicable of them all. It was popularised by rock stars and footballers (and Pat Sharp), and involved having your hair cut short on top, while growing it long at the back, so it usually hung down in lank looking strips like a nest of rat's tails. It wasn't so much a hairdo as a hairdon't – or indeed a hairdunnit (probably the barber, in the salon, with the rusty shears).

If you were more adventurous, you could add a perm to your mullet, spike it up on top and highlight it all over, thereby giving you multiple hairstyles, and yet no style, all at the same time. There were even special variations, such as the skullet, which was long at the back and bald on top (for slapheads who wanted a mullet) and the frullet, which was a long fringe and shaved at the back (like you'd put your mullet wig on the wrong way round).

The mullet was a clear favourite with heavy metal fans, who seemed to be under the illusion that it was somehow a macho thing. In fact it just made you look as if you should be wearing a

Pat Sharp's mullet was hair-raising stuff.

83

checked shirt, playing a banjo and drooling out of the corner of your mouth.

Thankfully the hairstyle eventually died out, although it remained popular in Germany for a long time after. In recent years it's managed to make something of a comeback. For anyone considering adopting this infamous haircut for whatever reason, may I recommend an alternative variant for your head? A bullet.

Naked Lady Pens   Novelty popular around 1965–85

The internet has made porn accessible to everyone these days, but before the web came along, if you wanted to see a pair of bare breasts belonging to a woman you hadn't actually married or plied with booze, you'd buy *The Sun*. Alternatively, if you wanted something a little muckier and could brave the newsagent's knowing smirk, you might purchase a copy of *Razzle, Penthouse* or *Playboy*.

But there was another way to look at the nude female form whenever you wanted to, and it was one that you could carry quite comfortably in your pocket. The naked lady pen was as much a part of the 1960s and 1970s as long hair and flares. When you held the pen the right way up or wrote with it, the modesty of the lady in question was perfectly preserved with a well placed swimsuit. But – and here's the clever part – turn the pen upside down and her swimwear would slide away, revealing a sexy woman in all her naked glory.

For kids who managed to sneak a look at their dad's pen while he was out of the room it was a revelation. Sadly it also set us up for years of frustration afterwards, when we discovered you had to actually unclip a bra to get at the goodies, not simply tip your date on her head. Whatever anyone else might tell you, space-age technology like this was the real reason we went to the moon.

Granted you needed to have bloody good eyesight to see anything worth ogling, and it was often hard to tell if you were looking at pubic hairs down there, or remnants of the chemical substance that hadn't fully drained away. They say that wanking makes you go blind, and back when a naked lady pen could well be your only source of titillation, that was doubly true.

Not that anyone would ever have used the pen for such a depraved act. Good Lord no. That's what the underwear section of the Grattons catalogue was for.

Nena

Germanic pop-princess Nena had just the one hit in the UK – the unfathomable "99 Red Balloons" in 1984. It was about the Cold War apparently, and told the story of the USA and the Soviet Union nuking each other after mistaking a load of balloons for an incoming attack. And in an ironic twist, lots of people mistook this load of bollocks for a decent song and it went to number one.

Of course, the main thing people really remember about Nena was that she had incredibly hairy armpits. When she lifted up an arm to point towards a cluster of imaginary inflatables it was like watching someone give birth to a baby gorilla.

Instead of selling poppies that year, the British Legion should have shown us pictures of Nena's armpits and explained that if we'd have lost the war, that's the sort of female foliage we'd be waking up to. I reckon they'd have broken all fundraising records with that line.

New Romantics
Music Subculture popular around 1980–84

Being a New Romantic meant being in touch with your feminine side. Growing your hair long, colouring it, styling it with enough hairspray to give Al Gore inconvenient nightmares, and wearing poncey clothes, like shirts with frilly ruffles, shirts with frilly sleeves, and pirate costumes. Frilly pirate costumes naturally. The New Romantics were a right bunch of frilly buggers.

Worst of all it meant experimenting with make-up. For most that meant slapping it on just as young girls do when they first discover mum's make-up box. Some went down the less is more route, with a little eyeliner and some lipstick, while others preferred the more is more

Like the old romantics, they wandered lonely as clouds. And it isn't surprising looking like that.

85

philosophy with foundation caked on inch-thick and patterns drawn on the side of their faces. Either way you looked a prat, although the latter approach was useful for avoiding being recognized by your skinhead friends when they were beating you up.

Naturally, the great experimenters of the movement were the New Romantic pop stars: groups like Duran Duran, Visage and Spandau Ballet. They were continually updating their images and coming up with new and ever more outrageous looks. Just as well, as no one would have been interested in them if all they had to offer was their music. You certainly couldn't dress that up as anything other than bloody rubbish.

Nik Kershaw — Pop Star popular around 1984–86

In his debut top ten single "Wouldn't It Be Good", Nik sang about how he thought the grass was greener on the other side, and how other people had it better than him. And they did. Mainly because other people – you know, normal people – didn't wear a snood, and thus weren't subjected to everyone pissing themselves with laughter every time they walked into a room. (A snood, for the uninitiated,

Good job no one ever took themselves too seriously in the 1980s.

was a cross between a scarf and a hood which made the wearer look like a cross between a knob and a tosser).

As if that clothing cock-up wasn't bad enough, he also tried to make fingerless gloves trendy. Legless trousers, he might have got away with. On account of the fact that they're shorts. But all fingerless gloves do is either make you look like a tramp, or someone who's so thick they don't realize that the sole point of gloves is to keep you warm – they simply shouldn't come in a summer variant.

He'll always be remembered more for his ridiculous fashion sense and shit hair than his music, but there was one song of his which caused much controversy. The title track of his 1984 album "The Riddle" was a perplexing enigma, the lyrics of which sounded like some sort of mysterious coded message or clever allegory on modern life. It talked of Babylon, seasons of gasoline and gold, and wise men saving America. Music journalists stayed up many a long night, drinking into the early hours and debating the exact meaning of Kershaw's poetic outpourings. Even today, my mind is still aflame with a burning question I'd desperately like answered by the pop star... What did you do with all your snoods, Nik? You twat.

Old Computer Games Video Games popular around 1979–90

Some people moan that modern computer games lack the playability of the old classics. How it's all graphics and sounds these days, with game play coming a very distant third. And you know what? That's absolute bollocks.

Computer games in the 1980s were shit. We just didn't know any better. Which is odd, because frankly we should have. When Sir Clive Sinclair rolled out the C5 we understood that while electric vehicles might have been the way of the future, what we were being offered there was a total joke. So how come we didn't notice when it came to video games?

The games themselves fell into distinct categories. There were platformers like Donkey Kong, in which you ambled along a platform, climbed ladders, collected items and avoided baddies or occasionally killed them. There were maze games like Pac-Man, in which you ambled around a maze, collected items and avoided baddies or occasionally killed them. And there were shooting games, in which you drifted through space, collected power-ups and avoided or killed baddies. To be fair, there were also some text adventures, where you typed in multiple unrecognized commands before being informed you'd been eaten by a mountain lion and were dead.

There were variations on these themes (collect eggs, collect stars, collect rings, collect keys), but they all boiled down to the same few concepts. The game play was universally easy to get to grips with, generally only requiring the use of a joystick and/ or a few buttons. To make it more challenging – and to ensure you didn't complete it in the ten minutes or so you would have otherwise – the designers routinely made the games rock-hard. Here's a ravine to jump over. Let's make it so you have to be standing on this exact pixel when you jump or you won't reach the other side. And let's have you being attacked by aliens with big guns at the same time. And, I know, let's make it so only one perfectly executed jump in ten actually succeeds.

The other trick to extend a game's life span was just to repeat the same levels over and over again, with perhaps a few different graphics and at a faster speed. "Bah, I got to level 57 of Pac-Man before being eaten by Pinky (or maybe Clyde) and now I've got to start all over again!" As if you could bloody tell…

So the old games were shit then, and they're even worse now. Load up a favourite title from the past on one of those ancient computers and see how long you play it for. My guess is you'll manage five minutes before chucking the ruddy thing out the window and firing up your Xbox 360 for some proper gaming fun.

Old Product Names — Brand Names popular around 1970–2005

Fat American Man: "Hey honey, I can't find a Snickers anywhere. There's a bar here that looks like it, in the same wrapper, with the same ingredients, by the same maker too, but it's called Marr-A-thon."

Fat American Woman: "Are you getting it, sweetie?"

Fat American Man: "Nah, come on honey, you know I only eat Snickers."

That's the reason Marathon was renamed to Snickers in the 1990s – it was the chocolate bar's overseas name and we didn't want to confuse or disappoint any American tourists. It's bad enough for them when they realize they can't just pop into Buckingham Palace for a quick cuppa with the Queen.

People harp on about how great the old name was, like it was part of our national heritage or something. Granted, Snickers sounds ridiculous, but Marathon wasn't much better when you think about it. What exactly did chocolate have to do with fitness? Bugger all. Presumably it was called a Marathon because that's what you needed to run to burn off all the calories crammed into its caramel and peanut laden innards. Basically, both names are shit, so why do people get so precious about these things? They're just names which can never hurt you, as the saying goes; either way the ingredients of the bar are exactly the same. If they'd have swapped peanuts for wingnuts, then sure, you'd have cause for complaint. Not that the customer service desk would be able to understand a word you were trying to say with a mouthful of bloody tooth fragments.

Loads of products have undergone corporate re-branding along these lines. Starburst is a crap name, but the original Opal Fruits was equally nonsensical. Dime Bar was too Yankee for our British tastes, so shops started stocking Daim bars instead.

The meaningless Immac brand became the equally rubbish Veet (I created my own slogan for it – "Veet! You stick it on your feet! And the long bit above your feet, you know your legs" – but it never took off). Oil of Ulay was always a stupid name for a face cream but shortening it to Olay was just plain unnecessary – unless their target market was actually Spanish bull-fighters. Jif also pointlessly altered its name by a single letter, and that caused untold confusion in supermarkets around the UK.

Old Lady One: "I can't find Jif anywhere and I need to clean my bathroom!"

Old Lady Two: "It must be here somewhere, I'll ask an assistant…"

[A few minutes later]

Old Lady Two: "He says Jif has changed its name to Cif!"

Old Lady One: "What?"

Old Lady Two: "He says he doesn't have any Jif, but he has Cif, Alice."

Old Lady One: "Speak up, you know I'm deaf. He has what?"

Old Lady Two: "He's got CIF, Alice!!"

Old Lady One: "SYPHILIS?"

Yeah, okay, maybe a name can hurt you. Especially if your girlfriend is on a neighbouring checkout.

Old School Dinners — Food popular around 1960–90

One of the great myths of our time is that school dinners used to be expansive platters of wonderfully tasty tucker. No, they bloody weren't. This is the sort of fare that was served up at schools back in the 1970s and 1980s…

Liver and onions. Bloody liver, which tasted like old shoe leather and was harder to pass than 'A' Level Physics. Spam fritters which resembled fried road-kill. Impossibly lumpy mash potato which was so solid it had to be carved out with a stainless steel ice-cream scoop. Watery semolina, also known as vomit pudding. Custard which didn't so much have a skin as a fucking crust complete with shifting tectonic plates.

Okay, so the school dinners of yesteryear had marginally more nutritional value than the current platefuls of sickly yellow bread-coated sweepings from the abattoir floor some kids get these days. Being the lesser of two evils isn't exactly much of an achievement, though.

And incidentally, a word to my hairy lipped battle-axe of a dinner lady, Mrs Haddon – that kidney and offal pie didn't make me grow up into a big strong lad. It did however make me throw up into a big strong bin liner.

89

Operation

The key to successful operating procedures is a steady hand. Of course, it's also handy to have a patient whose nose lights up red when you take out the wrong kidney. That's exactly what happened when you made a surgical faux-pas in this Milton Bradley game, which featured a mock operation involving tiny plastic organs.

The board was an operating table with a bloke called "Cavity Sam" drawn on it, who had holes cut into his body containing the various plastic organs. Each player would take a turn at extracting an organ with a pair of tweezers – if they touched the edge of the hole, the chap's nose would illuminate and a buzzer would sound, indicating their failure. Unlike the real world, however, a malpractice lawsuit didn't follow swiftly in the post. One problem with the miniature playing pieces was that they were easily lost or indeed swallowed. Eventually, so many went missing that Operation became like playing poker with a deck of ten cards. Also, the anatomical information imparted by the game was woefully inaccurate, which didn't help adolescent would-be doctors.

Since when has a patella been shaped like a bucket? Or an ankle bone like a spanner? MB was clearly extracting the urinary tract here. A further blatant failure on the realism front was the omission of one of the most common surgical procedures – where was the rectal cavity, with a small plastic light bulb piece ensconced within it? In fact, it's surprising they never produced an adult version of the game – they could have called it Operation: Gynaecologist (featuring "Chlamydia Chloe"). Although such a game would doubtless have confused male players no end. Differentiating between two sets of lips – none of which could whistle – would have been hard enough, let alone the nightmare of locating the tiny clitoris piece without the owner co-piloting ("left a bit... up... up... no, that's my bellybutton...").

Orville

"I wish I could fly, right up to the sky, but I can't." You see that's the thing with wishes. Some come to fruition, others don't. I personally wished that the bastard duck would disappear, and luckily it came true. Quite what Orville is up to these days I've no idea. All I'll say is green duck à l'orange tastes as disgusting as it sounds. Like eating fuzzy felt, in fact. I'd guess Keith Harris, the man with his hand permanently wedged up Orville's backside, tastes like chicken though. He and his crap ventriloquist act always were foul.

Oversized Cards

Back in the 1980s, there were cards for people who wanted to say Happy Birthday! And there were also cards for folks who preferred to say HAPPY BIRTHDAY! Giant three foot long cards with eight inch lettering and an image of a teddy bear that was more the size of a real life grizzly.

These crass oversized cards were popular with the big egos around at the time – the sheer magnitude of the thing was a statement of how much you loved your significant other. Even if you clearly didn't love the Amazonian rainforests.

God forbid you actually posted one of them. They played havoc with sorting machines, and the last thing you wanted was one of these monstrosities rolled up and jammed in your letterbox. It made your door look like it was smoking a massive spliff, especially when the hoodlum kids from next door set fire to it. It also caused problems down at immigration, who doubtless eyed any air-mailed people-sized envelopes very suspiciously, just in case the Czech really was in the post.

Panini Stickers

During the 1980s, at break-times all over the country every schoolboy would huddle together, heads bowed, studying intently. Not books – naturally – but something else. All you could hear across the playground were low voices saying: "Got, got, got, got, got, need, got, got, got, need, need…"

Nearly everyone collected Panini. Not the Italian sandwiches, but the football stickers. You lived and died by your stack of "swapsies." The stickers were purchased in packets of five and stuck into an album, with every team having its own double page spread. Swapsies were the duplicates you got, that you'd try to exchange with other kids for stickers you still needed.

Completing your album almost became an obsession. You'd spend all your pocket money on the daft things in the hope that you'd get that rare Ian Rush sticker, or even better, a badge. These golden or silver team crests were the most prized because they were all metallic, mint and shiny, and on the playground stock exchange, a Manchester United badge could be worth as much as two Mars bars, a quarter of fudge and a Beano annual. Depending on the early morning market movement and the volatility of midget gems.

After countless hours of negotiations and barter, doing deals with your mates, zealously hunting down rare badges, and spending tens upon tens of pounds on packs of stickers, you'd finally place the last sticker in the album with your breath held, carefully making sure it was lined up and all square.

Then you'd be instantly bored with it and chuck the stupid thing in the back of your wardrobe somewhere, never to be seen again.

As adults, we can all look back now and wonder how a company managed to make a massive success out of publishing a picture book without any pictures, and then charging people to enter a lottery to win the pictures. I'm only surprised they didn't leave the words out and have packs of letters on sale down the newsagents as well.

Pan's People — Dance Troupe popular around 1968–1976

In the days before video, *Top of the Pops* consisted mainly of acts miming along to their current chart hit. Which was fine, so long as the singer or group in question could get to the studio on the day of recording. If they couldn't, it would be left to Pan's People to provide a three minute visual accompaniment to the music instead.

Pan's People was an ensemble of fit young women whose job it was to interpret songs through the medium of dance. Often literally. "Bankrobber" by The Clash saw them pretending to carry out a bank raid, which at least made sense. Lip-synching Gilbert O'Sullivan's "Get Down" to a group of bemused dogs was one of their less obvious efforts. Lord knows what they'd have made of Elvis Presley's "Wear My Ring

Pan's People brought new meaning to the word interpretation.

Around Your Neck", but you wouldn't have bet against it involving them shoving their heads up some giant inflatable arses.

Whether they were any good or not is a matter of debate. Some of their performances were certainly cringe-worthy, but that didn't really matter because their real role was eye candy. In those days a group of lovely ladies cavorting around in sprayed-on hotpants was as close to porn as it was possible to find on TV. Dads and teenage boys alike tuned in every Thursday at seven, hoping that James Brown didn't feel good (and hadn't got on up), Stevie Wonder had got lost on the way and Yes had said no.

Eventually Pan's People were replaced by Legs & Co. and then Hot Gossip. The idea was much the same, just with different dancers. In the end the groups were phased out and replaced by the pop video, many of which are now filled with girls wearing less clothes than Pan's People would have worn in the shower. Oh and you know how I said it was a matter of debate whether Pan's People were any good or not? The only real debate was which of the dancers you'd "do" first. And believe me, there was no shortage of guys desperate to have Pan's playing on their pipes.

Parka
Winterwear popular around 1975–85

The original Parka was the king of winter coats at school. In fact, it looked more like Arctic trekking gear, with its padded insulation and large hood, which was fur-lined for that authentic Eskimo appearance. The traditional British Parka was blue, with a bright orange inner lining, and the hood came right up over your head. It was possible to zip the hood fully up, so it covered most of your face, just like Kenny from *South Park*.

The Parka – the ideal coat for introverts everywhere.

This was cool, as you could pretend you were a periscope, or perhaps some sort of weird furry faced alien, or even Captain Scott, ready for an expedition through the thick snow. There were a few problems with the coat, though, all of which revolved around that hood.

Many kids were fond of putting the hood on, but not the coat itself, so it flapped behind them like a cape as they ran around pretending to be in an episode of *Batman*. All it took was for some clown to grab the trailing Parka and it'd quickly turn into an episode of *Casualty* with a dose of third degree whiplash.

Another downside was that when fully zipped up, the hood could be grabbed by a bully and scrunched shut, completely encasing your head so that you could barely breathe. Then, if he was in a really bad mood, he could jerk you forward so you fell over, and pull you around the playground by your head.

Finally, the hood was obviously a road safety hazard, as it effectively blinkered kids. It was damn difficult to follow the Green Cross Code without any peripheral vision. Tufty never wore a Parka, after all. Mainly because he was a squirrel.

So, hoods off to the good old Parka, the coat of extremes. When wearing one, you'd be lovely and toasty warm. Either that or stone cold dead.

Phone Cards — Calling System popular around 1982–95

It used to be the case that if you wanted to phone somebody while walking down the street you'd go into a payphone, get some change out of your pocket and make the call. Easy. But then BT came to the conclusion that it was losing too much money through vandalism and suchlike, and decided that getting us to pre-pay for our calls would be a better idea. Thus the phone card was born. Like a credit card, but for phones, it could be used to make unlimited calls anywhere in the world for ever and ever. Or until your credit ran out at least.

What this new system actually meant was now when you wanted to phone somebody while walking down the street you'd go into a payphone, stare hopelessly at the card slot, look in your wallet for a card you knew you didn't have, pat your pockets forlornly for a card you knew you'd never purchased, and then go off in search of a shop which sold them or a phone box which accepted coins.

As an incentive to get people to buy more cards BT even started customising them to make them collectable. And naturally collectors fell for this ruse and started hoarding the bastard things – making them an even rarer commodity.

"Do you sell phone cards?" "Yes we do."

"Great, I've been everywhere. Can I have a £5 one please?"

"The limited edition Princess Diana card? Sorry mate, just sold the last one to a collector."

"Bollocks. Okay, I'll have a £10 card please."

"The classic engineering Triumph TR6 card? Sold out I'm afraid."

"£20?" "D-Day Landing? All gone mate."

Three cheers for the invention of the mobile, that's all I can say. They might have annoying ring tones, a bunch of features you never use and cameras designed purely for recording happy slappings, but at least they let you make a phone call without needing to mug a passing card collector first.

Platform Shoes — Footwear popular around 1970–77

You have to wonder what the hell the point of platform shoes was. Wearing them didn't make you look big or clever, just tall and stupid. Though I guess they were useful for short people who could instantly gain a couple of inches and be seen as being fashionable rather than, say, a short arse overcompensating for lack of height.

Platform shoes were, like most 1970s fashions, very dangerous. Or perhaps that should be highly dangerous. Moving around on them was more a matter of tottering than walking, running was risky, and dancing in them was definitely to be discouraged. Not because of the probability of injury, but just because there's nothing more embarrassing than a man disco dancing

They had the dancefloor to themselves. Strangely enough.

in three inch blocky heels. Platforms were incredibly unsafe shoes. You could easily slip and end up laid flat out on your back (the only way you'd get laid wearing them). If you were really unlucky, you might twist or even break your ankle, which had disastrous consequences for the fashion minded. Especially as, despite numerous requests, the NHS steadfastly refused to introduce platform plaster casts.

Pong

"Anyone fancy a game of Pong?" It was the cry of insomniacs everywhere. Pong was the game that, if played properly, never ended. You would control one paddle, your friend the other, and a small square ball would bounce between the two. You could, if you were very good (or very lucky), get the ball to bounce off the corner of your paddle, adding "spin" which made it much harder to return. Although the only time your opponent would miss it was when they lost concentration for a second or two, or got up to go to the toilet.

Pong was available to play in fairground arcades, but also at home. Systems like the Binatone brought the boredom of the first popular computer game into the living room. To help make Pong more interesting – and it needed all the help it could get – some hardware developers thoughtfully added a fiendish twist in the shape of super-sensitive controls. This involved making the dial you used to manoeuvre the paddle so light that turning it just one millimetre in either direction would be enough to shoot your bat right to the top (or bottom) of the screen.

Instantly the simplest game on the planet was transformed into the hardest. If you and your friend both really concentrated you might manage (after a couple of hours) to get a score that just broke into double figures, which was a serious achievement. As an added bonus you gained all the skills you needed to be a master safecracker along the way, so it wasn't all bad.

The home systems also came with several variations of the game, so as well as Pong you could play Tennis (Pong with a line in the middle of the screen), Squash (Pong with walls) and Breakout (Pong with breakable walls). They were either dead easy or impossible to play, depending on the system you owned. They all had one thing in common though. They were universally crap. Pong by name, pong by nature.

Protect and Survive

The Cold War led to a pretty frosty atmosphere between the superpowers, but it was nowhere near as chilling as the government's information films advising the public what to do if nuclear war broke out. *Protect and Survive* was narrated by a posh bloke (actor Patrick Allen) and it told you how to protect your family and therefore survive. Although it didn't mention purchasing a lead-lined basement bunker with a direct lift from your penthouse flat, like Allen probably owned.

What average people needed, apparently, was a fall-out room. This wasn't a room where mum and dad went to argue out of sight of the kids because he'd been down the pub until 2 a.m. again, but an area central in the house and therefore furthest away from the walls and roof. The further you were away from the outside atmosphere, the harder it was for fall-out radiation to penetrate and affect you. Bungalow dwellers were pretty much fucked, but then again, they were mostly pensioners, so only had a 50/50 prospect to last out any given week anyway, nuclear war or no nuclear war.

It wasn't enough to just have a fall-out room – for extra protection you also needed an inner refuge inside it. This was constructed out of doors leant against the wall, with mattresses, suitcases or any other padding you could find strapped to them. Inside this double layer of protection, you'd be invulnerable to radiation. Because, apparently, mattresses soak up gamma rays like they absorb piss. And suitcases can survive a trans-continental British Airways flight, so a global thermonuclear war should be no problem.

However, *Protect and Survive* missed a couple of key tricks in keeping away the spectre of radiation sickness. How about family members taking it in turns to blow towards the windows, helping to repel any gamma-laden dust particles? Or making a radiation suit out of tin foil and a pair of swimming goggles? The government probably made other disaster information films they never got round to airing. Such as *Defend and Don't Die*: Protect yourself from a chemical weapons attack by wearing a clothes peg on your nose, and carrying several large suitcases around with you to block any vents or openings that gas might potentially seep through.

Or perhaps *Swim and Don't Sink*: Protect yourself from a tidal wave by strapping a lilo to your back and holding a large suitcase out in front of you to absorb the dangerous hydrogen and oxygen particles you'll be bombarded with. Maybe even *Resist the Reckoning*: Survive the arrival of Revelation's apocalypse by climbing inside a large suitcase. In the middle of a mattress factory. Owned by God.

Punk — Music Subculture popular around 1977–79

In the late 1970s, the disaffected youth of Britain received a rallying cry in the shape of punk rock. This was raw, fast, rebellious DIY music, very different from the bland, polished and melodic disco which had been popular up until then. You couldn't dance to it, but you could jump up and down on the spot and claim to be dancing, which made it great for anyone with two left feet. Or a pogo stick.

Bands like The Sex Pistols, The Clash, The Damned and The Stranglers embodied the spirit of punk and soon the movement spread countrywide. Suddenly it was cool to wear safety pins again – for the first time since growing out of nappies – and you could dye your hair any colour you liked. Except maybe medium brown. And you could spit. In fact, not only could you spit, but you had to. If you didn't gob everywhere, especially over your mates, then you weren't a real punk. You also

Who you calling a stereotype? Fuck off before I gob on you.

had to swear a lot. Johnny Rotten had done it on the telly so that made it okay to f-and-blind in Sainsburys while shopping for tofu with your parents, or during a visit to see Nana in her nursing home. Eventually, The Sex Pistols split up, people got bored of listening to crap shouty music, and punk turned into new wave, then the New Romantics arrived. After a few more fads disco returned as dance. It was, many people lamented, as if punk had never happened.

I'm not so sure. The spirit of punk was all about bands that couldn't really play their instruments, singers who couldn't sing, and rubbish songs. The look and the attitude was all that mattered. Sounds an awful lot like *The X-Factor* to me.

Quatro   Drink popular around 1982–85

In 1982 an exciting new soft drink was launched. Quatro was a mix of fruit flavours carefully blended together to create an instantly forgettable taste. It came in a can with a large stylised letter Q printed over the top of four coloured squares representing the different flavours of the drink. There was orange (for orange), yellow (for lemon), red (for cherry) and green (for washing up liquid).

Suzi Quatro shared the same name as the drink, and in 1973 had a hit called "Can the Can", which proved to be very prophetic when Quatro was indeed canned a mere few years into its short life. Coincidentally, Suzi's career also went flat in the 1980s, which just goes to show how cruel the pop business can be.

Rah-rah Skirt

"Does my bum look big in this?" is one of those questions which sounds as if it should have a multitude of possible answers, but for which there is actually only one proper response and that's a resounding "No!" Any other reply isn't merely dicing with death, it's taking a six-sided cube and shoving it up his nasal socket while simultaneously dissing the size of the bony fellow's scythe.

There is, however, one exception to this rule. If the woman asking you the question is wearing a 1980s fashion faux-pas like the Rah-rah skirt (or its equally flouncy cousin, the puffball skirt), you then have two possible answers at your disposal.

"Does my bum look big in this?"

"Yes. Christ you look like Big Bird!"

Or:

"Yes. What the fuck have you got on?"

Red Phone Boxes

For some people the increasingly rare red phone boxes are sacred. They're like the Holy Grail of British life as it used to be. Except this particular grail never held the blood of Christ, just the piss of old tramps.

Reliant Robin

There were several advantages to owning a Reliant Robin. Because it was a three-wheeled vehicle, you only needed a motorcycle licence to drive one, and it was much cheaper to tax. You certainly didn't need to worry about being asked to give someone at work a lift home either – there was no chance of anyone willingly being a passenger in that particular vehicle. Never mind robin red breast, you'd be robin red face if anyone saw you clambering out of one.

The Reliant Robin was as embarrassing as it came. Its nickname "plastic pig" made it sound much cooler than it actually was. Even Ogle Design, who created it originally, recognized it would only appeal to certain types of people. Its design codename was TW8, perilously close to what drivers of the car found themselves being called whenever they took theirs out on the road.

Rod Hull and Emu — Act popular around 1975–90

Who could forget that shocking moment in chat show history when a bird suddenly attacked the unsuspecting host. The assault came with no warning (just a curled lip beforehand) and was vicious, unprovoked and left the poor old chap befuddled and slightly distraught afterwards. Russell Harty certainly never invited Grace Jones back after that performance. It was a similar story when Emu attacked Parkinson, ravaging him with an avian death-grip around the neck.

Emu always seemed very cross and bad tempered, but then again, if you had a Rod up your arse constantly you probably wouldn't be a barrel-full of laughs either. Ultimately, however, it wasn't really Emu that got the raw deal, but poor old Rod who was constantly overshadowed by the feisty blue bird. When it came to the double act's TV programmes, it was *Emu's World* not *Rod's World*. And *Emu's Broadcasting Company*, not *Hull's Broadcasting Company*. Not to mention *Emu's Pink Windmill Show*, although in that particular case *Rod's Pink Windmill* sounds like something very scary which certainly shouldn't be shown to kids.

In the 1990s Rod fell into obscurity, and in 1999 he fell off the roof of his house while adjusting the TV aerial, with fatal results sadly. Emu's still occasionally on the television today, so evidently survived the fall. Not sure how, given he's a flightless bird.

Roland Rat — Puppet popular around 1983–87

I'm sorry, but when the best thing about your breakfast show is a mangy rat puppet with an annoying voice and an entourage consisting of a baby rat, a guinea pig, a hamster and a gerbil, you really shouldn't feel pleased with yourself.

Roland Rat was introduced to *TV-am* when the show was dying on its arse in

1983 ("the only rat to join a sinking ship" was the comment). Two million viewers were consequently added to the viewing figures. Whether the show's recovery is entirely down to him, it's hard to say, but if so that's a staggering amount of loonies with access to remote controls. In reality, the viewing figures were probably bolstered by a large amount of children tuning in. What a great way to save a dying news-based breakfast show – turn it into a pre-school programme for kids.

Given how successful his introduction apparently was, you have to wonder why this approach hasn't been repeated since. *Eldorado,* BBC1's ill fated and piss-poorly acted Spanish soap might not have failed if the powers that be had introduced Sid Slug and his friends Sally Snail and Bert Bumblebee when the ratings started to tumble. And if Mr Blobby had moved into *Brookside,* he could easily have saved the show from the axe. Mind you, communication could have been a problem there. Poor old Blobby would never have understood what those Scousers were going on about.

After saving *TV-am,* Roland and Kevin, Errol, Little Reggie and Glenis transferred to the BBC where they starred in some purpose-made shows, including *Roland Rat: The Series.* This was great, but only because it said exactly what the programme was about so you could easily avoid it. Unlike *TV-am,* which should have come with a warning, but didn't.

Roland also released five singles and two albums. Anyone who says today's music is rubbish should be forced to listen to "Rat Rapping". The follow-ups were even more harrowing. Worst of all, Stock, Aitken and Waterman were responsible for one of the singles and some of the tracks on Roland's second album. They probably thought that was about as low as their music careers could possibly sink. But two years later they were working with Jason Donovan, which I guess made their time spent with a rapping rat seem like something of a high point.

The only "Rat on the Road"
I want to see is a squashed one.

The Roly Polys  Dance Troupe popular around 1982–90

Les Dawson was a great comedian, but he's got to take some flack for introducing the Roly Polys to the world. This group of fat middle-aged female dancers first appeared on his show in 1982 and went on to perform in a number of light entertainment programmes in the 1980s – despite the fact they were blatantly neither light nor entertaining.

The joke, if you can call it that, was that dancers are normally stick thin and these wobbly food scoffers weren't, so – get this – they couldn't pull off all those fancy steps without looking cumbersome. The newsflash that fat people couldn't bend over very well and weren't particularly lithe was tear-streamingly hilarious. The whole thing certainly made me cry, anyway. For multiple reasons.

The Roly Polys were so successful they even toured the globe, which was quite an achievement… For the airline that managed to get a plane off the tarmac with the entire troupe on board. They even made it big in the Far East, although it's hardly surprising they were welcomed there. The harpoon-happy Japanese have traditionally enjoyed watching whales flounder around dying.

Sometimes they say a stage can't hold a performer. Always a worry for the Rolys.

Of course, the Roly Polys had their admirers back home, as well. As a porky Pan's People, they were a chubby chaser's wet dream, and doubtless they had groupies queuing up outside their dressing room doors. The overweight ladies probably got lucky on many a night, providing it wasn't the wrong time of the month. Even hardcore fans of these large puddings would be unlikely to want to tuck into a jam Roly Poly.

Ronco — Gadget Maker popular around 1970–83

Ronco is still going even now, but its heyday was unquestionably the 1970s, when it churned out a seemingly never-ending range of unnecessary and frankly pointless "time-saving" gadgets. Its initial range of products included Chop-O-Matic (a self-circumcising kit), Dial-O-Matic (which rang your ex-girlfriend for you whenever you'd had too many drinks) and the Veg-O-Matic (a comfy seat in front of the telly). Oh alright, these were all products for slicing and dicing your food.

As the company grew, it added more and more odd and obscure products to its range. There was the Miracle Brush (you tried it, realized it was shit, threw it out and on the third day it came back from the bin), the Glass Froster, the Smokeless Ashtray, the In-Egg Scrambler, the Record Cleaner, and the Bottle and Jar Cutter. The latter was a guillotine designed to turn old glassware into attractive, very cheap, razor-sharp vases for the home. The 1970s was such a classy decade.

Two Ronco products stick in my mind best. Firstly, there's the legendary Buttoneer. This was a stapler for buttons. When a button fell off, instead of sewing it back on, you used this device to re-attach it with a plastic staple. The point was to say goodbye to tedious button-sewing and save yourself time and effort.

Now I don't know about you, but I really don't have that many buttons falling off on a regular basis. In the 1970s, it was clearly a major problem. Maybe cotton was made out of delicate spider web gossamer back then, which simply dissolved whenever you tried to do anything too strenuous with it. Such as fasten a shirt or a coat. That's the only reason I can think of for the Buttoneer's ludicrous popularity. "Arrgh, another button's fallen off! That's the 112th this week. It's no good, we're going to have to buy one of those fancy button staplers, Barry."

The other gadget that warrants a mention is the Trim-Comb hair groomer. This was a comb with a razor blade inside it. You (or your parents) combed it through your hair and the device gave you a smart trim, thereby saving a few pence on a proper haircut. At least that was the theory. In reality what happened was mid-way through a session your mum or dad would get distracted by something, but keep combing anyway. When they finished you'd look in the mirror and see they'd done a great job. Of making you partly bald.

In later years, Ronco capitalized on its product's popularity for introducing pre-teen boys and girls to premature male pattern baldness by launching GLH (Great Looking Hair), a spray-on toupee designed to cover up any bald spots. But seeing as that didn't actually arrive until the late 1980s, it meant freshly scalped children of the 1970s had just two choices. They could either go to school entirely shaved and blame their new look on an outbreak of nits, or they could have their missing hair clippings glued to their heads in a haphazard and truly embarrassing manner. As "Tufty" Tomlinson will no doubt tell you.

Rubik's Cube   Toy popular around 1980–83

The Rubik's Cube is a puzzle. The puzzle being, how the hell did it become so popular? After its official launch in 1980 the famous toy, which is a cube divided into sides of three-by-three coloured squares, exploded with unbelievable sales. Mine exploded when I chucked it against my bedroom wall, but that's another story. In its first three years on the market, over a hundred million cubes were sold, and the damn thing's still selling today. The idea behind the Cube was that you mixed up all the coloured squares, and then had to twist and move the blocks around, to get all the squares of the same colour back on the same side. Except what actually happened was you tried that for a couple of hours, planting the seeds of RSI in your wrists, then got thoroughly pissed off with the whole thing, peeled the coloured stickers off and just stuck them back on in the correct places.

The trouble was, once you'd "solved" it this way a couple of times, the stickers would start to peel, lose their stickiness and fall off, leaving you with a rather dull matt black cube. Which was an interestingly nihilistic modern art statement about the darkness of ever-turning eternity, perhaps, but a bloody crap toy.

The Saturday Starship   TV Programme popular around 1984–85

In 1984 Big Brother was watching us, but whatever little brother was watching it wasn't this load of ITV Saturday morning twaddle. *TISWAS* had originally been replaced by *The Saturday Show,* but it was so rubbish the producers needed to come up with a great idea to save it. Unfortunately, they came up with a shit idea instead – set the programme inside a space craft and rename it accordingly. The fact it only managed one series should tell you how woeful it was.

Tommy Boyd was inept at best on *The Saturday Show,* but here he really shone. Not because he'd got any better, but because he'd been given Bonnie Langford as his co-presenter. What were they thinking? Charley the cartoon cat from the public information films would have been a better choice. Even his non-stop yowling would have been considerably less irritating than bouncy Bonnie's screeching tones.

Everything that's ever been transmitted on this planet is slowly making its way across space. If our TV broadcasts ever reach an alien world, two things could happen depending on which programme they tune in to. If they catch an episode of *Star Trek: The Next Generation,* they'll think we have a very well armed and organised space fleet, and any invasion plans will be quickly forgotten. Should they see *The Saturday Starship,* and Captain Bonnie Langford teaching a crew of children a dance routine, they'll launch an attack to wipe us out immediately. Not just because they think our fleet will be a pushover – we'd also blatantly deserve it.

Scalextric

Toy popular around 1960–90

Brrrm! Brrrm! Vrroom! The idea of having a race track with self-powered cars to bomb around it is an absolute dream come true for most little lads, hence the enduring appeal of Scalextric. The toy featured cars driven along slots in a track by electric motors (which also powered headlights if you had a fancy set), and it was high on most kids' Christmas wish-lists. Sadly, as always, the reality fell far short of the dream. The adverts featured a sweeping long track with bends and chicanes galore, and four Porsches swishing round like greased lightning, pulling level with each other and battling for pole position going into the last corner in an adrenaline pumping finish which got the players' hearts pounding.

In real life, you played with a small and unexciting oval course with a single chicane, or , if you were really lucky, a modest figure-of-eight. Despite this compact nature, it still took your dad a while to set the stupid thing up, as the bits of track were quite fiddly to snap together, particularly when your Scalextric was getting on a bit and had been stood on and bent in places. Then you raced two cars for approximately five seconds until one of them came off the track because it was going just a touch too fast round a corner.

So you had to get up and put it back on – it almost always departed the course at the corner furthest away from you – then five seconds later another vehicle would be off again. At least the toy delivered on its promise of heart pounding action. Ten solid minutes of constant standing up and sitting down and not only was your heart going like the clappers, you were starting to get a headache.

Never mind burning rubber, when playing Scalextric you were more likely to be smelling singed carpet, as that's where the cars spent the majority of their time.

Screwball
Ice Cream popular around 1970–90

The Screwball was the ice cream with half the fun – you could eat the contents, but not the cone, as that was plastic. Unless you were descended from that weird French bloke who ate light bulbs, in which case you could presumably tuck in happily.

To make up for this shortcoming, there was a ball of gum in the bottom of the pot – the Screwball the name was derived from. It was so called because once you started chewing it, you realized you'd been screwed over, as it tasted like some dire chemical concoction of additives, and it was invariably cold and soggy.

To make matters worse, this crap gum was so thick and impliable, to get a bubble out of the stuff you needed lungs like a champion marathon runner, a tongue as dextrous as a viper's, and the blowing skills of a Dutch hooker. Even then, a successful result would be about the size of a pea, at best.

There was one positive thing about the Screwball – once finished, the empty container made a pretty good approximation of a toy Dalek when turned upside down. You could argue the realism was rather ruined by the lack of Dalek appendages, but I'd disagree. Every Screwball came with its own sucker attached, in the form of the kid who'd bought it.

Sea Monkeys
Brine Shrimp popular around 1960–2008

Harold von Braunhut was a bloody liar. In fact he was a serial bloody liar. And worst of all he peddled his lies exclusively to impressionable young children through the medium of American superhero comics. No, he wasn't responsible for making us believe that a man could fly, or that dressing up like a giant bat would make you look anything other than ridiculous. What Harold did was advertise toys. The problem was his products didn't exactly live up to the claims that he made for them.

His range included X-Ray Specs that couldn't see through anything and Invisible Goldfish which weren't so much invisible as, well, entirely non-existent. And then there was Sea Monkeys. These weren't available over here (not in any real quantity), but we could read about them in astonishment. They were like creatures from another world. How we envied the American children who could actually cut out that magical coupon and send off for those astounding animals…

The lies surrounding Sea Monkeys are legion. They aren't monkeys for starters. They don't live in the sea either. Just salt-water lakes. They don't, as the large colour advertisements suggested, live in family units – mum, dad and the kids – they aren't humanoids, and they don't play by leapfrogging over one another. In reality, they are nothing more exciting than dehydrated brine shrimp, also known as *Artemia Salina* (or *Artemia NYOS* these days). More at home in a fish bait shop than a toy shop.

The dishonesty didn't end there either. According to the adverts they were three eyed freaks of nature, a bowlful of happiness, instant pets – "the most adorable pets" no less – who were so eager to please they could even be trained! They'd obey someone's orders like a school of tiny dolphins. And seem to dance when music was played to them. And they grew really quickly too, reaching the size of half an inch in just twenty-one days and yet they lived for over a year! So how large could they get? At least eight inches in size surely? And their owners would never tire of them. Ever!

All bullshit of course. The shrimp did come to life magically when you tipped them into water, which was quite impressive. And they would follow a beam of light from a torch. But trained? The most adorable pets? No. They were water fleas, hardly in the same league as a cute puppy or a fluffy kitten. And the size they reached in twenty-one days was as big as they ever got. Thankfully. And children would never tire of them? They lost interest in the rubbish things the moment they discovered Sea Monkeys looked nothing like the creatures in the adverts. To be fair, if they'd checked the small print they'd have seen the ads did say the caricatures shown were "not intended to depict Artemia Salina", but everyone knew that. They were intended to depict Sea Monkeys. Artemia what?

The first sizeable shipments of Sea Monkeys took until the 1990s to arrive over here and are still available to buy in most toy shops today. If you want to get some for your children, be sure to show them the adverts for months beforehand to build up their expectations. The true Sea Monkeys experience is built entirely around crushing disappointment.

And while you're in a buying mood, can I interest you in a packet of Walkers Sea Gorilla Cocktail crisps? They make the most adorable pets…

Shake 'n' Vac — Carpet Freshener popular around 1980–88

The idea behind Shake 'n' Vac is brilliantly simple. You sprinkle some perfumed powder over your carpet, then vacuum it up, leaving nothing behind but a nice smell. Or as the once-seen-never-forgotten advert from the 1980s explained it:

Do the Shake 'n' Vac, and put the freshness back,
Do the Shake 'n' Vac and put the freshness back,
When your carpet smells fresh, your room does too,
Every time you vacuum, remember what to do…
Do the Shake 'n' Vac and put the freshness back.

The ad involved a happy housewife in a voluminous white skirt (and stripper heel shoes) dancing around her living room demonstrating how to use the product. I reckon if they remade it today they should approach Amy Winehouse for the role. If anyone has experience of uncontrollable shaking and hoovering up copious quantities of white powder, it's definitely her.

Shakin' Stevens — Pop Star popular around 1981–85

Unbelievably, in a decade full of men in make-up, dyed hair and frilly shirts, the best-selling singles artist of the 1980s was a bloke who thought blue denim was still the height of fashion. Shaky's anachronistic brand of rock 'n' roll took him to the top of the UK charts three times and earned him the nickname "the Welsh Elvis." Which sounds impressive, but when you actually think about it is probably on a par with being one of the Peterborough Beatles or the Geordie Jesus ("Ha'way Lazarus man! Get gannin' ya lazy shite").

His real name was Michael Barratt, but he was called Shaky because he was born with cerebral palsy which he suffered from until a chance visit to Newcastle (not really). He had loads of hits including "Oh Julie" and "You Drive Me Crazy", although some of his biggest numbers referred to what I theorize might have been his back-up profession. As one of Britain's pioneer property developers.

"This Old House" might have been sung about a run-down place he picked up on the cheap. But he didn't have time to fix the shingles, or repair the floor due to his pop commitments. His insistence on "Green Doors" didn't help either. Neutral colours, Shaky, neutral colours! There was, however, a bigger potential sales problem. Who'd want to buy a Barratt home?

Shoulder Pads — Fashion Accessory popular around 1980–89

These days the majority of women aspire to be slim. Some want to be stick thin, while others would be happy enough to just shed a few pounds or drop a dress size. Back in Thatcher's 1980s, it was a different story entirely. Women wanted to be powerful and look powerful, so they bolstered their feminine frames with American Football style shoulder pads.

Jackets had them sewn in, as did blouses. (Bras sometimes did, but the padding was generally rather lower down). Everywhere you went there were women who looked as if they were about to play in the Superbowl. And the bigger the big hair got, the bigger the shoulder pads had to be to balance everything. Really fat women, with massive shaggy dog perms had shoulder pads so wide they had to strip off to fit through doors. There was a lady on our street who wore

Eek: what (Dy)nasty shoulder pads she's wearing.

a green jacket with the largest, bulkiest shoulder pads ever produced. She thought she was at the cutting-edge of fashion, a power-dressing goddess with broad shoulders that could take on the world. Which is kind of odd really; to us kids she just looked like the Incredible Hulk having a bad hair day.

Sinclair C5

Sir Clive Sinclair was an inventing genius in the early 1980s. The man who gave us the pocket calculator and the ZX80, ZX81 and Spectrum home computers could do no wrong. He was like an egg-headed Midas, everything he touched turned to gold; although with his electronics bent, it was more like silicon. If he could still pull off that trick today, he'd have glamour models queuing up outside his house to let him have a quick feel of their assets.

When he announced he was turning his attention to electric vehicles, you could almost smell the fear emanating from the petrochemical industry – for a suitable contemporary parallel, imagine peace threatening to break out in the Middle East. Shares in BP and Shell fell to an all time low. Well, all right, maybe I'm exaggerating a teensy weensy bit.

In January 1985, the first launch from Sinclair Vehicles was rolled out. It would have been driven out, but frankly they couldn't find anyone thick-skinned and stupid enough to clamber into the three-wheeled embarrassment. Priced at £399 (plus £29 P&P), the C5 had arrived. It was quickly ridiculed by everyone who saw it. Except motoring organisations like the AA, who were slightly more concerned that the battery-assisted tricycle might, quite possibly, be a death trap.

Given it could be purchased by anyone, didn't require a licence to drive on the road and involved the user sitting a mere two inches off the tarmac below, they had a point. Going over the Niagara Falls in a barrel was a potentially less hazardous form of transport. And a much faster one, too, seeing as the Hoover-produced C5 had a top speed of 15 MPH on the flat, increasing to about 70 MPH when going downhill attached, in a mangled fashion, to the undercarriage of the speeding juggernaut which had just ploughed over it.

In the end only around five thousand C5s were ever sold, most of them ending up in service as wheelbarrows (albeit pretty damn funky and futuristic looking ones).

Hands up if you feel like a complete arse.

When astronaut/test pilot Steve Austin crashed an experimental spacecraft into the ground, it cost his employers an arm and a leg to get him fit and well again. And another leg. Not to mention a cybernetic eye.

As the show's weekly intro explained: "Steve Austin – Astronaut. A man barely alive. Gentlemen, we can rebuild him. We have the technology. We have the capability to make the world's first bionic man. Steve Austin will be that man. Better than he was before. Better... stronger... faster." And presumably not half as shit at landing prototype spaceships.

Since he clearly didn't have insurance to cover his seven-figure hospital bill, the improved Steve signed up to work for Oscar Goldman at the OSI (Office of Scientific Intelligence), where he put his new superhuman abilities to good use in a James Bond style.

Every episode's plot followed the same theme. At some point Steve would have to look at something in the distance using his bionic eye, break a padlock (or similar) with his bionic arm and then run somewhere really fast with his bionic legs. Well, that's what they claimed he was doing. Rather than showing him running at a hundred miles an hour, his super-fast sprints were portrayed as slow-mo jogs instead.

It was pathetically unconvincing even at the time, but at least it ensured the number of accidents at school decreased massively for the few years the programme was broadcast. Come break-time, every child under the age of twelve would be running incredibly slowly around the playground. And making odd Bwawawawa-nnnnaa-gggggghh noises – the sound Steve's bionics made when they kicked in. You'd have thought that six million dollar price tag would have covered the cost of a can of WD-40.

The success of *The Six Million Dollar Man* led to stacks of merchandising and an inevitable spin-off. After a skydiving accident, Jaime Sommers (Steve Austin's girlfriend) received two new legs, a new arm and a new ear to become the Bionic Woman. Given that she was quite flat-chested it's surprising that the people rebuilding her didn't take the opportunity to bolster her frame with some bionic breast implants. They'd have looked superb bouncing in slow-mo when she went running. And after the series ended she could have nabbed a lead role in *Baywatch*.

Steve and Jaime weren't the only recipients of bionics. There was Barney

Miller, the Seven Million Dollar Man, Andy Sheffield, the Bionic Boy, and even Maximillian, the Bionic Dog. Thankfully, the show came to an end before we had to endure the sight of Hammy, the Bionic Hamster, rolling around the floor in his plastic orange hamster ball and bowling the bad guys over like skittles in ludicrous slow-motion...

Smurfs   Cartoon popular around 1978–85

Ahh, the Smurfs. Kids' cartoon stars extraordinaire. Who could forget them? Actually, who could remember them, there were so bloody many. There was wise old Papa Smurf. And, er, Happy Smurf. Grumpy... and Sleepy... Dozy... Dave, Beaky, Titch, and, erm, Harold. Oh and the girl one of course. Over a hundred blokes inhabited Smurf village and there was just Smurfette to go round. Jesus, no wonder she was blue. And she never emigrated either. The slut.

The Smurfs were also sold as toy figures, but they were particularly crap ones. They didn't have eagle eyes or lightsabers you could put in their hands. You couldn't even look up Smurfette's skirt. And instead of Tie Fighters, their accessory toys were things like mushroom houses. Fungal abodes which didn't shoot laser beams, or have buttons you could press that made cool noises. Rubbish!

The blue people also sang – although not the blues, surprisingly. They sang happy ditties, to keep themselves smiling, and to remind each other of their lofty communal ideals. But mostly they sang because droves of sponge-headed prats bought whatever soppy old cobblers they happened to spew onto vinyl, and incredibly, even in later years after their popularity had diminished, the CDs were still selling.

The Smurfs Go Pop (they go crackle as well if you douse them in lighter fluid and apply a naked flame) made the UK album chart in 1996. It contained classic tunes such as the ripped-off "Mr Smurftastic" and the horrifying cross-breed "Mr Blobby and the Smurfs". The moment the fat pink plastic twat met a load of small blue dicks could have been truly orgasmic if only someone had inserted a freshly lubricated nuclear warhead into the proceedings. The resulting meltdown would have been Smurfing brilliant.

In fact, the Americans genuinely wanted to nuke the Smurfs, as the Bible-belt hardcore believed that the magical elements of the stories were satanic references. Religious types probably spent many a Sunday afternoon playing their Smurf records backwards, listening carefully for subliminal demonology. They never discovered any, but did find out that the music sounded 100% more palatable this way.

The Smurfs have also been accused of being propagandists for communism, with their classless, share-everything society. Wackier Smurf conspiracies have even suggested there are parallels with the Ku Klux Klan, on the basis that almost all of the Smurfs wore white hoods, but notably not Papa Smurf, their leader, who had a red one. And KKK officers happened to don a red hood. Hmm. Thinking about it, the Smurfs did spend a lot of their time dancing around blazing fires in the woods. Maybe that's why the only black Smurf was the chimney sweep.

But even if any of these wild allegations were true, their greatest crime would still be the fact that the bloody "Smurf Song" was the fifth best-selling UK single of 1978.

The Snood — Clothes popular around 1980–90

The snood might sound like some sort of monster out of *Doctor Who*, but it was in fact the 1980s equivalent of the hoody. However, it was even more ridiculous looking, basically being a cross between a scarf and a hood which was worn over the head. I'd love to have been in that fashion concept meeting:

"Yeah, it's like a scarf, but the clever bit is, it's got a hood attached."

"Right…"

"So in winter it keeps both your neck and your ears warm."

"What does it look like?"

"It keeps your neck and ears so toasty warm you wouldn't believe!"

"But what does it look like?"

"The Eskimo market are so going to go nuts for this!"

They got the moniker wrong at any rate. Given that it's a hybrid between a scarf and a hood, the abbreviation really should have been scood. Although truth be told, the most convenient name for this fashion faux-pas would simply have been "Twat." That would have killed two birds with one stone, as when you pointed out "that twat over there", you'd be succinctly naming the head-gear and owner in one fell swoop.

Sodastream

"Get busy with the fizzy" is what the adverts used to urge in the Sodastream's heyday. And what a fantastic and tantalising idea it was for kids – a pop making machine which you could use to produce your own Coke, all summer long. This was the theory anyway – you took some plain old water, put it in a special bottle, inserted that into the machine and carbonated it, a bit like Darth Vader did to Han Solo in *The Empire Strikes Back*. A concentrate flavour could then be added to the fizzy water, such as cola, orange or lemonade.

However, there were two problems with the resulting beverage. Unless you gulped it down immediately, it began to lose its fizz swiftly and generally it would go flatter than a supermodel's chest around halfway through your drink. Secondly, it tasted like shit. Cola flavoured Sodastream simply did not taste like Coke. It tasted like you were chugging a watered-down fizzy Fairy Liquid. Just like every other flavour.

But the Sodastream wasn't all bad. If you pressed the button too much and over-fizzed your beverage, it made hugely entertaining and incredibly loud farting noises that no human armpit could compete with. And you could experiment with the machine, although it was even more unstable than your average junior chemistry set.

If you used a non-standard bottle, there was a danger it would explode under the pressure. And if you carbonated some milk or other miscellaneous liquid, it would foam up and fountain all over the place. The same thing would happen if you added the concentrate to the water before the fizzing process, and sticky syrup would spray everywhere. You'd have to explain to your mum that the brown gunk all up the side of the fridge wasn't a dirty protest – better that than having to drink the sodding stuff.

Sooty and Sweep

Without a doubt, Sooty was a bloody cheat! Or rather his owner was. While the likes of Keith Harris actually had to do some ventriloquism work with his daft duck Orville, Matthew Corbett (and father Harry before him) needed bollock-all talent to operate his completely silent sidekick. A fortunate coincidence indeed.

Sooty wasn't actually mute – he could still talk to Matthew by whispering in his ear. He was just a very shy puppet, and I'm not surprised. If a bearded prat was fisting me on a weekly basis on national television, I'd probably be pretty damn embarrassed too. And it's no wonder Sweep did all that squeaking.

Space Dust

No one ate Space Dust because it tasted nice. In fact, most people probably couldn't tell you what it tasted like. It wasn't intended to be savoured though. The idea was you put the synthetic sherbet into your mouth and then you went round opening and closing your gob while it exploded on your tongue. Well, it popped and fizzed anyway.

When you had your mouth closed it made a weird echoey noise inside your head as if aliens were trying to contact you through the medium of static electricity. And when you opened your mouth it could be heard from miles away. Or by people standing next to you and listening intently, at least.

When you swallowed the stuff you could feel it continuing to make its way down your throat for ages. And some people even claimed they could feel it popping away in their stomachs, but they were talking bollocks.

On its own Space Dust was fairly harmless, but if you ate enough of it and drank a few cans of fizzy pop, it could cause your stomach to explode. Or so the urban legend had it anyway. Just as well that turned out to be a load of rubbish, otherwise we'd have some interesting suicide bombers to contend with:

"Sarge, it's Fatty Patterson. He's eaten thirty packets of strawberry Space Dust."

"So what? He's a fat kid, they eat a load of–"

"And he's threatening to down four cans of Coke in quick succession if we don't hand over the keys to the tuck shop…"

"Jesus Christ! The kid's a walking time bomb. Give him whatever he wants, and in the meantime you'd better evacuate the entire school…"

Space Hopper

First seen in this country in 1969, the hopper was an inflated rubber sphere which you sat on and bounced along the pavement, holding on via two rubber handles (which looked like horns, as the toy had a strange and freaky face painted on the front). The space part of the name suggests that you could emulate zero-gravity and bounce in huge hops, but the reality was you could perhaps reach about a foot high if you were lucky. And about half a foot if you were fat. If you were asthmatic as well as fat, it made a good seat.

As a method of travel, it was slower than walking, and it lacked a little something in the comfort stakes. Actually it lacked a little everything. All that bouncing hurt your arse after a while, and it could make the more sensitive little tykes feel a bit sick. They were also quite easy to fall off – a well aimed kick from a bully in mid-hop could be devastating. Plus there was always the (admittedly unlikely) danger they could explode if over-zealously inflated.

So they were uncomfortable, slow, pointless, potentially explosive and crippling. Well that just about ticks all my fun boxes, it's no wonder they were all the rage throughout the 1970s. I suppose we should just be grateful they weren't radioactive, even though they looked it in that lurid orange colour.

The one single thing that the Space Hopper was actually good for was something its designer definitely didn't have in mind: Twatting your brother over the back. It made a lovely hollow thwacking noise and bounced off at great pace, sometimes even hitting you in the face on the rebound. So for comedic violence it was great – but for anything else, the Space Hopper was simply a very orange waste of space. Just like Dale Winton today.

Space Invaders   Video Game popular around 1980–83

The first real arcade game, Space Invaders revolutionised trips to the local fair. Instead of hanging around the dodgems, kids started loitering in the arcade section. The game was straightforward enough – rows of green aliens would wobble slowly back and forth across the screen, dropping down one row every time they reached an edge. The player had to shoot them. While the concept sounds fine, in reality the game was tedious beyond belief. It was the digital equivalent of watching slow-motion raindrops trickling down a dirty windowpane.

When the game first started, the computer's weedy CPU would labour to move all of the aliens at once. As a result they crawled across the screen at a speed more associated with glaciers than gaming. You moved along the bottom at a reasonable pace, certainly fast enough to avoid the sluggish alien bullets, but you could only fire one shot at a time. Your lone bullet would go upwards until it hit an invader or reached the top of the screen and vanished. Then you could fire again.

The whole time the game boomed out a sound effect reminiscent of a beating heart, presumably to remind the player that he was indeed still alive. It was only as you started to eliminate aliens, thereby giving the CPU less work to do, that the invaders began moving at a challenging pace. Even so it was still bloody BORING.

If aliens really did invade Earth and they were like these bleeders, we wouldn't have much to worry about. Technologically superior they might be, but by the time they'd lowered their way through the stratosphere, we could have organised the entire human race to collectively turn out the lights, switch off their televisions, draw the curtains and pretend not to be in. Eventually Space Invaders got replaced by a new generation of games. Space shooters like Galaxians which took the same concept but added multi-direction movement, speed, colour and entertainment to the mix. They were still shit but the challenge was now how long you could stay alive, not how long you could stay awake.

Speak & Spell   Toy popular around 1980–85

This educational toy looked like a computer for kids, with a colourful plastic keyboard and a dinky fluorescent display above it. All it did, however, was let you play a range of simple spelling games, the main one of which was the spelling challenge. As the name suggested, it spoke a word, and you spelt it – er, spelled it – erm, typed it in on the keyboard. The sales gimmick was that Speak & Spell was a machine that could talk, just like a real human being. Well, just like a robot anyway. A robot with android laryngitis. And a rusty brain – it… spoke… veh-rrry… slowww-lyyy. Think Stephen Hawking on dope.

At least the famous scientist and author is perfectly comprehensible. Sometimes with Speak & Spell, the challenge wasn't spelling the word, but understanding what the bloody hell the word was. For example, you'd be asked how to spell "Enza" and after pressing the repeat word button about ten times and straining to listen really carefully, you'd eventually work out that you were actually being asked to spell "Answer." Speak & Guess & Spell might have been a more apt name for the machine.

It wasn't all bad though. I guess Speak & Spell might have helped children with learning difficulties better understand the art of spelling. Or maybe not…

"Now spell: Dyslexic."

"D-I-L-S-L-X-E-C-I-C."

"Incorrect." (Sound of machine smashing against wall).

Spot the Ball   Competition popular around 1980–90

Back in the days before the National Lottery was even a twitch in Camelot's lance, there were other nationwide gambling schemes. Most of which seemed to revolve around football, like the pools, which is still going today, and Spot the Ball, which isn't – not in any meaningful form anyway.

The idea of Spot the Ball was simple. A newspaper printed a freeze-frame photo of an action moment in a football game and removed the ball. The reader then had to mark where he or she thought the ball was. They could also draw a comedy moustache on Emlyn Hughes, although that was entirely optional. The key to Spot the Ball was to think outside of the box. Well outside of the box in fact, as the football would rarely be anywhere near the 18 yard area – or anywhere else you might expect it to be. When the results came back in the next week's paper, you'd curse the air blue when you discovered that the referee had shoved it up the front of his shirt, or it had rolled off into an unlikely looking corner of the pitch while every player's eyes were fixed on a streaker just out of the picture frame, or a low-flying pigeon.

What was it about the bloody players? They never seemed to be looking anywhere near the ball. Did the competition panel purposefully pick out the most cross-eyed, boggle-goggled footballers, or did they sit in the stands themselves when the snaps were taken, reflecting mirrors into the player's faces?

Or maybe, and this is just a total stab in the dark – often the best way to find the missing ball – the footballers were given a cut from each week's game to deliberately gaze in the wrong direction or leap to head a ball that was actually sitting stationary by their feet. After all, in those days players didn't get paid millions a year, so playing Spot-anything-but-the-Ball would have been a good way to supplement their income. That's probably why the game has died out in recent years. The only players they can find to go along with it now are in the Conference league, and trying to find an action moment to photograph in one of those matches is like attempting to locate a clean portaloo on the last day at Glastonbury.

Status Quo   Rock Group popular around 1972–86

Status Quo means "the existing state of affairs" in Latin, which rang pretty true in the band's glory days – they definitely existed in a fair state, what with their long lank hair, scruffy denim jackets and dubious guitar skills. The myth goes that Status Quo only ever had three chords, but that's a downright lie. They had four, actually. Rick Parfitt occasionally wore a pair of brown ones. After all, it was the 1970s.

The Quo penned a number of top ten hits throughout that decade and well into the 1980s, from "Pictures of Matchstick Men" to "In the Army Now". They're probably best remembered, however, for opening Live Aid in 1985 with the seminal "Rockin' All Over the World". And when I say seminal, I mean it was a pile of wank.

After the mid-1980s, their popularity went into decline, although the band are still making, if not really selling, albums – a somewhat disconcerting fact now they're on the verge of drawing their pensions. Never mind "Rockin' All Over the World", I'd be happy if they'd just rock off.

Sticky Back Plastic — Self-adhesive Material popular around 1960–80

Some brands enter into the public consciousness so deeply they eventually end up becoming generic. Hoover, for example, is another way of saying "vacuum cleaner." Every vacuum cleaner in Britain is a Hoover. Even if it's a Dyson. You might be drinking a Pepsi but you're still enjoying a Coke. There are loads of brands like this: Sellotape, Biro, Band-Aid, Google…

Then you have the exact opposite. Brands which, for one reason or another, fail to make any impact whatsoever or worst of all end up being called something entirely different. Fablon for example. Or to give it a name you might actually recognize, sticky back plastic. Fablon was championed throughout the 1970s by *Blue Peter*, but because the BBC programme didn't do brands, it never got a name check. So the great British public rushed out to buy sticky back plastic instead.

This material came in a variety of colours and patterns – none of them tasteful. Which in the 1970s, the decade of the avocado bathroom suite, was just what people wanted. There was even a particularly unimpressive wood-effect version complete with unconvincing grain.

Few products were as ubiquitous as sticky back plastic. A single roll of the durable, waterproof self-adhesive material could be used for anything. You could make *Blue Peter* projects from it – an Action Man lunatic asylum for example – as well as cover various items of furniture, ranging from chairs and tables to televisions (although not the screen, obviously). It could even be used to decorate your schoolbooks. I've never heard any mention of sticky back plastic covered cars, but nothing would surprise me.

People would cover their dining room chairs with it, and then – when they fancied a change – paint over it. When they fancied another change, they'd cover the whole thing in another sheet of the bloody stuff. And, here's the most amazing thing of all – every single one of your visitors would think it was cool. The height of contemporary elegance.

"Ooh, are those new chairs?"

"No, they're the old ones but I covered them in cheap self-adhesive plastic sheeting." "Really? But they're fabulous. Is that a new oak table?"

"Sticky back plastic again."

"You're joking! But it's got knots in it and everything."

"Yes, but it's knot wood." "Ha ha."

About the only thing you couldn't cover in Fablon was a human being. Shame really. If they'd worked at making the material a bit more breathable, a whole new range would have opened up for the future. Sheets with hair printed on them could have been used to fashion sticky back toupees and chest wigs, and the right muscle layout would give you an instant six pack stomach. You could even use the material to get the looks of a Hollywood star. With a weird, stretched plastic face you'd be a dead ringer for Nicole Kidman.

Stock, Aitken and Waterman — Music producers popular 1984–90

In the late 1980s, the charts were awash with songs written and produced by Mike Stock, Matt Aitken and Pete Waterman. They worked with everyone. Seriously. They weren't in the slightest bit discerning. Yeah, they wrote for Bananarama, Rick Astley, Kylie Minogue and Jason Donovan. But they also did stuff with Viz comic's The Fat Slags, Roland Rat, Pat and Mick, Sam Fox, The England Football Team, Cliff Richard, Sigue Sigue Sputnik, WWF Superstars and Bill Tarmey – Jack Duckworth off *Coronation Street*.

The hit factory – one letter missing from what should have been a spot on nickname – managed to churn out an incredible number of tracks, many of which were hugely successful. Cleverly, rather than actually writing new tunes they just repeatedly regurgitated the old ones. A change of lyrics, someone different to sing them, and hey presto it's a whole new song.

If an infinite number of monkeys were given an infinite number of typewriters and an infinite amount of time (not to mention an infinite amount of Tipp-Ex) it's theorised they'd eventually reproduce the works of Shakespeare. Similarly, if an infinite number of monkeys were given an infinite number of synthesizers and twenty minutes, they could probably reproduce all the hits of Stock, Aitken and Waterman. Having said that, you'd hope they'd have the good taste not to bother.

Stylophone — Musical Instrument popular around 1970–80

Played using a stylus, hence its name, the Stylophone was an electronic instrument with a unique sound. When you pressed the pen-like tool against the all-metal keypad, you were treated to a noise that sounded like a cross between a hive-full of angry bees trapped inside a megaphone and a farting robot.

By sliding the stylus over the different notes you could play any monotone song you knew the tune to, although there was no guarantee that your listening audience would recognize it, or that you could find anyone prepared to be a listening audience. Most sensible people would scarper the moment a Stylophone appeared in the room. Rolf Harris was the advertising face of the instrument, which was a good choice, given that anyone playing one was obliged to ask "Can you tell what it is yet?" halfway through any song.

The answer would always be the same mind you. "Yes, it's a bloody racket. Turn it off will ya?"

Unbelievably, you can still buy Stylophones and torture people with them today, which seems like one hell of a loophole in the Geneva Convention.

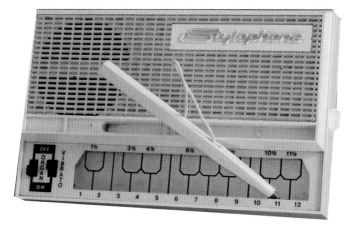

Jabbing the pen in your ear would've been more aurally palatable.

Subbuteo was indeed a beautiful game. It was a highly detailed world of toy football – you could buy stands, plastic fans to sit in them, electronic scoreboards, floodlights that worked, all manner of accessories which made the environment impressively realistic.

As a simulation of football, it was pretty spot on too. If indeed real football involves standing around for most of the match, with your feet cemented into a concrete block, staring at a ball which is actually bigger than yourself. Which it most likely does – if you play for a Sunday league police informant's team of midgets.

Subbuteo was played by flicking the players at the ball and knocking it forward, hopefully into the opponent's net. You kept possession until you missed the ball, or it hit an opposition player.

Come and have a game if you think you're hard enough.

That was the theory, anyway. However, because this was rather dull for the passive player, most games devolved into you and your mate furiously flicking multiple players simultaneously at the ball and eventually having a fight. Which, I suppose, simulated the hooligan elements of footie quite adeptly.

This always happened when I played, because the game was so bloody boring otherwise. You see, the fun of Subbuteo wasn't actually playing it, but collecting all the different teams and their strips, along with the many accessories.

As your collection expanded, your Subbuteo set became a thing to be admired, not used, which was just as well because by the time you'd built up the North, South, East and West stands, and corner terraces, TV towers, plastic advert hoardings and manager's dugout, not to mention the toy cameramen, linesmen, ball-boys and policemen cluttered on the side of the field, you couldn't actually get near the pitch to play even if you wanted to.

Superhero Outfits — Costumes popular around 1975–85

As a youngster, I thought I was a superhero, but I knew I didn't really have super powers. I knew I couldn't fly, although I could lie across a chair, arm extended in front of me, and pretend. I knew I couldn't shoot red laser beams out of my eyes, but I could pick my nose and flick a green projectile into the girl next door's hair.

However, I also knew that everything would be different if I had the proper costume. If Father Christmas would bring me a real Superman outfit like the ones in the catalogue, there would be no stopping me zooming around the Earth 15 times a second and reversing time back to the start of the summer holidays.

If only. Sadly, all children's superhero outfits were purposefully made of the cheapest material available, which must have been some sort of hybrid between tissue paper and PVC. One exploratory leap off the top of the garden fence and you'd split your red pants around the crotch. Superman himself never had these problems – he might have had trouble with kryptonite, but never a poorly stitched seam.

Plus, God forbid you ever decided to confront the school bully, with delusions that your new clobber would allow you to punch him into next lunchbreak with your super-strength. When he'd finished laughing at you, he'd get you in a headlock, and thank you kindly for wearing your pants on the outside where they were so much more conveniently accessible for wedgie purposes.

Sweat Bands — Fashion Accessory popular around 1983–86

Sweat bands were designed to be worn by sportsmen in order to prevent sweat from their foreheads dripping into their eyes. They were especially popular with tennis players, footballers, basketball players and Jane Fonda when she was doing one of her workouts. Oh and with Mark Knopfler from Dire Straits for some unfathomable reason. They also briefly and terrifyingly became popular with some sections of the great British public, who started buying and wearing them, along with matching wrist bands, in places where there was no danger of ever sweating. Like air conditioned pubs for instance.

The hope, presumably, was that simply wearing sweat bands like this was enough to convey the image that they were athletic, sporty types without their needing to actually go to a gym or do any form of exercise. "Well, you know, I think I'm pretty fit. I try to wear my sweat band at least three times a week for an hour or so. And last week when I took it off it was quite damp. It was raining fairly heavily at the time though…" This delusion was doubtless augmented by a lack of blood to the brain, since as well as preventing sweat from trickling into your eyes, the towelling band also doubled as a pretty effective tourniquet.

Sweet Cigarettes — Sweet popular around 1930–80

Like sweet tobacco, that other smoking-inspired confectionery product, sweet cigarettes were a treat for children that no one thought bad at the time. They were best consumed on a frosty morning, because when you exhaled, you could pretend your condensed breath was real smoke. The fact that they might inspire kids to take up smoking wasn't considered to be a big deal, because smoking wasn't something that was considered to be a big deal. You grew up, and you tried ciggies. If you liked them, you stayed with them until you developed lung cancer, or you didn't.

Sweet cigarettes were white sticks of candy with a splodge of red at one end representing the lit part. They came in a rough facsimile of a fag packet, and even had collectable cigarette style cards in them, but unlike the real thing the government didn't take a huge chunk of the price in tax. If that had been the case, you'd no doubt still be able to find the sweets in the shops.

Mind you, if they were still on sale today they'd probably have been joined on the shelves by other similarly unsuitable products. Alcoholic lemonade, cola or Irn Bru for example. Ha, the very idea!

TaB — Drink popular around 1970–90

An early version of Diet Coke, TaB was so called because it helped people keep tabs on their weight. Apparently. Underneath the name the packaging on the can boasted about how few calories it contained. All of which makes me think TaB was actually an acronym – Tastes Awful But… only 2 calories!

There were several versions of the drink made, most notably TaB Clear which was a colourless cola. No calories, no colour, no cola taste… Maybe it should have been called TaP. Water.

Tales of the Unexpected — TV Programme popular around 1980–88

Back in the day, TV didn't actually have to be good. The fact that miniature people moved around inside a box in your living room and you could watch them – in colour – was pretty impressive. You didn't need incisive scripts or clever ideas back then, you could make any old shite and people would watch it. And this maxim still held true in the 1980s to some extent. I mean, people tuned in to *Tales of the Unexpected*, and Lord knows why. The tales (the early ones being based on Roald Dahl's short stories) were supposed to be chilling and macabre affairs with a twist, but they were about as unexpected as Jade Goody failing to finish the London Marathon.

Because it was called *Tales of the Unexpected*, you expected the unexpected, which then became the expected. Then everyone got very confused, went and made a cup of tea and just tried to forget the whole thing (easier said than done).

The most unexpected element of the whole shebang was the quality of the actors they managed to rope into this low budget crap-o-rama (names like John Gielgud and Derek Jacobi). How they managed that remains, to this day, a genuinely unfathomable mystery.

Through the Keyhole — TV Programme popular around 1983–95

In the history of film and television we've heard some ridiculous accents. Keanu Reeves' attempt at an English one in *Bram Stoker's Dracula* for example, or Dick Van Dyke's comedy cockney in *Mary Poppins*. But neither of these comes close to Loyd Grossman's bizarre accent. The original presenter of *Through the Keyhole* sounded even more laughable than those awful fakes.

The pretentious prat's inimitable nasal slurring became a trademark of the programme, along with his catchphrase "Who would live in a house like this?" – to which the obvious answer was "Piss off Loyd, you wanker."

The show was all about poking around a guest star's house, and it was quite popular back when it first aired simply because people are nosey bastards. It was a big novelty in the 1980s (there was no *MTV Cribs* back then). Once the viewers and a panel of barely D-list celebrities had been shown the tour of the home, they had to guess who owned it, which was invariably some other complete nobody of a semi-celeb. It was all quite shockingly pointless.

And yet, unbelievably, *Through the Keyhole* has limped on through the years. Grossman has long since left, thankfully, but what the format really needs to pep up viewing figures is a cutting-edge revamp for the twenty first century. Might I suggest *Through the Arsehole*. A minor celebrity is given a colonoscopy, and the panel get to watch the camera's exploratory journey up through the bowel. Any takers? D-listers will happily spend weeks locked in a house with Jade Goody in the name of reality TV, so a spot of anal trauma should be a trifling matter in comparison.

Maybe Shilpa Shetty would go on it (the subtitle for that episode could be "A Passage to India"), Julian Clary ("The Tunnel of Love") or Loyd Grossman himself. There's no joke there, it'd just be fitting revenge for his past presenting. And I'd definitely rather see his shit than listen to it.

ThunderCats   Cartoon popular around 1985–90

In the 1980s we were inundated with rubbish imported cartoons. There was *Battle of the Planets, Transformers, Dungeons & Dragons* and of course *ThunderCats*. The fearsome felines in this show originally came from a planet called Thundera but then their home world moved house one day and they had to find somewhere new to live. Or it exploded. I'm not sure which. Travelling across the universe, probably in a cat basket, they endured skirmishes with mutant bandits led by the mummified Mumm-Ra, suffered fur balls, and had to cope with a shortage of scratching pads. Eventually they arrived on a planet called Third Earth where they had lots of exciting and somewhat repetitive adventures usually involving the evil Mumm-Ra who certainly lived up to his nickname "the Ever-Living" by refusing to die. Even the episode where they put him in a bag with a load of bricks and threw him in the canal didn't do the trick.

The ThunderCats comprised of a tiger called Tygra, a panther called Panthro, a lady cheetah called Cheetara (such imaginative names), two kittens called WilyKit and WilyKat and a twat called Snarf. I don't know what he was supposed to be, but he was bloody irritating.

Their leader, however, was Lion-O. The giraffe. All right, so he was a lion, who wielded the powerful Sword of Omens. This legendary weapon granted him "sight beyond sight", which basically meant he could view anything through its hilt. This was damn useful for spying on Mumm-Ra, watching football matches from outside the stadium, and having a quick shufty under Cheetara's leotard.

Of all the cats, it was Cheetara who stood out the most, and not just because she was easily spotted (yuk yuk). She was in fact the only adult female cat on the planet, which I bet made her popular when she was on heat. Sure, she could outrun every cat there if she chose to, but she never did. No wonder every time Lion-O saw her, he would hold his mighty weapon in both hands, point it in her direction and shout "ThunderCats, Ho!"

Tight Fit — Pop Group popular around 1981–82

Tight Fit had three top ten singles, but there's only one that people can actually name – their number one cover version of "The Lion Sleeps Tonight". The hit before that was called "Back to the 1960s" and was a Stars-on-45 style medley of 1960s hits. It reached number four, so they bashed out a quick follow-up called "Back to the 1960s Part 2", which scraped in at number thirty-three and necessitated a change in direction. One that was to alter the face of British pop… forever!

Or the face of the group at least. The video for "The Lion Sleeps Tonight" introduced the world to band members Steve Grant, Julie Harris and Denise Gyngell for the first time. Steve looked like a male model and sang the song in such a high pitched falsetto it left the world in no doubt that the Tight Fit of the band's name referred to his underpants. Thanks in no small part to its catchy intro ("Ee-ooo-ee-ooo, ooo-ee-ooo-ee-oh, ee-ooo-bums away! Ee-ooo-ee-ooo, ooo-ee-ooo-ee-oh, ee-ooo-bums away! Wimoweh, a-wimoweh, a-wimoweh…") it was a smash hit and Tight Fit looked guaranteed to have a long and successful chart career.

But then the follow-up came out. "Fantasy Island" managed number five. It was a straightforward ABBA rip-off and for this song Steve chose to wear a tight-fitting headband in the video and sing the track in someone else's voice. Even getting the girls to sing more, and louder, couldn't disguise the fact that something dodgy was going on. According to some individuals in the know, the group hadn't actually sung a single note of "The Lion Sleeps Tonight" (not even one of the 'ooo's). It was all session musicians. Could this be true? And if it was, could we believe anything the band said any more? What if the lion wasn't actually asleep? What if he'd never been asleep? What if there was no lion? It was all too awful to contemplate. After the accusations of lip-synching foul play it was downhill all the way. The group split up and we never really heard from any of them again. Although Denise Gyngell did have one more flirtation with a pop fiasco. She married Pete Waterman.

Tiny Tears

 Toy popular around 1965–85

Quite possibly responsible for a global increase in teenage pregnancies, Tiny Tears was (and indeed still is) a realistic baby doll that cried tears and wet itself when given a drink of water. It was exactly like a real new-born in every detail. Exactly. Aside from the whole not-howling-the-house-down-when-it-cried part of course.

Tiny Tears fooled millions of girls around the world into thinking that looking after an infant was, well, child's play. Small tears would dribble down its perfect plastic face, but yet, stoically, it made no noise whatsoever. Not a single whimper. It didn't yell, it didn't shriek, it didn't even gurgle. Babies are easy to look after, its silence said. Why not have one today? You'll hardly even know it's there. And look, babies piss tap water too, so you don't even need to change its nappies – just stick it somewhere warm for a bit and it will dry in a couple of hours. What could be easier?

Tiny Tears was such a success that manufacturer Palitoy looked for new ways to make more money. They rolled out clothes, potties and baby baths but still missed a massive opportunity if you ask me. If they'd have adapted the design slightly they could have produced a Tiny Tears capable of excreting warm chocolate sauce and done a deal to flog packs of doll-sized Pampers to all those junior mums-in-training.

Yes, it would have made the dolls a little harder to look after, but fat kids would have lapped it up. Literally.

Palitoy also managed to boost its profits by producing the dolls in other sizes. Alongside Tiny Tears (regular) there was Teeny Tiny Tears (smaller), Teeny Weeny Tiny Tears (smaller still) and Itsy Bitsy Teeny Weeny Yellow Polka Dot Tiny Tears (made up). However, I reckon they missed another opportunity – surely making the dolls bigger was the way to go, with obese babies or better still, conjoined twins. They could have charged twice the price for that one.

Tiny Tears cried buckets. As did parents when they discovered the cost of accessories.

Tortoises

Back in the 1970s, people were bored of cats and dogs and craved more exotic pets. Birds like parrots, toucans and cockatoos enjoyed increased popularity, as did colourful snakes and weird ugly fish. The most unlikely new pet, mind you, was easily the tortoise.

A slow moving, greenery-munching creature which divided its time between ducking its head inside its shell when frightened – every time you went near it or picked it up – and hibernating, it was hardly the most thrilling of pets to give to a child. The pet rock came into fashion in America at around the same time, and as stupid as that was, children probably got far greater pleasure out of caring for a lump of granite than they ever did a tortoise. Assuming they could tell the difference.

The reason for the reptile's popularity was twofold. Firstly, the shell which covered its back was perfect for painting. You could draw what you liked on it, or cover it in sticky back plastic. Writing the word "Fuck" on the school tortoise was always fun, as was daubing it with swastikas and placing it on your head while pretending to be a Nazi soldier.

The other main reason for the tortoise's meteoric rise was *Blue Peter*. The show was responsible for introducing an entire generation to the joys (limited as they were) of the prehistoric pet. The programme's first tortoise was called Fred. His name was emblazoned on his shell and the world fell in love with him. Well, the UK did anyway. Then it was discovered he was a she, and children everywhere tuned in to see a letter "a" being added to the end of his name. It was the world's first televised gender reassignment. After Freda came Maggie and Jim, then geriatric George and finally Shelley (ha ha – can you see what they did there?). The names might have changed, but their roles on the programme rarely varied. Typically, they would be brought out in front of the cameras once a year, only to be placed in a cardboard box and forced to hibernate. It was thrilling stuff. You know when the most exciting thing you can do with a pet is prepare it for a long winter snooze, you're not exactly going to have a wild roller-coaster ride of a relationship.

Tortoises can generally live as long as people, but few in the 1970s did. A diet of lettuce leaves, fish fingers and space dust, coupled with enforced and extended hibernation meant that 90% of the poor creatures died within two years. It got so bad that eventually the government was forced to step in and ban their importation in 1984. You can still buy tortoises these days, although there's little real point. A crushed beer can painted greeny-brown with a dog turd sticking out through the ring pull makes for a much cheaper and more pleasurable substitute.

Trivial Pursuit  Game popular around 1983–87

Trivial Pursuit made it massive in the 1980s. The trivial knowledge quiz game was perfectly timed for a decade which was ultimately about show-offs. Everyone flaunted everything, whether it was their big hair, overdone make-up, sports car or indeed their knowledge of Bolivian Weevil farming.

"Triv" as it was known (or "Twiv" if your name was Tarquin) was a game that always brought up loads of questions – about the questions themselves. Do you have to give a person's Christian name as well as their surname to get the answer right? (This tended to vary depending on whether it was a crucial "cheese" question – the cheese-shaped segments you had to collect to win the game). Is it fair that you got a question wrong because the person who read it out pronounced something incorrectly?

Other classic arguments included: "You only got that one right because we've had it before," which would swiftly be followed by accusations of somebody taking the questions from the wrong end of their box. Or there was always the immortal: "You could never have known that, you saw the answer on the back of the card as I picked it up!"

Let's not forget the old standby: "That answer's wrong, I swear! Let me get my encyclopedias out…" Trivial Pursuit was essentially 50 different ways to have a petty argument, and at the game's end, when you'd landed on the central square with all your cheeses collected, only the final question would remain: Why the bloody hell are we playing this shite?

The favourite game of the personality challenged.

UB40

When they first started, UB40 were a political band, highlighting the plight of the unemployed through the medium of reggae. It's a bit of a shame they didn't choose to do it through the medium of mime, really. It would have made their message so much easier to listen to.

The group's name was taken from the form you had to fill in to claim unemployment benefit (Unemployment Benefit Form 40), their first album was called *Signing Off*, and one of their early singles was "One In Ten", which was the jobless statistic at the time. UB40 didn't just sing about unemployment though, they did their best to combat it by employing as many rubbish band members as they possibly could. Forget duos or four-piece groups, there were eight people in UB40. Quite what they all did I doubt anyone could say – but whatever it was, it sure as hell wasn't write good songs.

They went on to have hits dealing with a wider range of topics, but all of their number ones were cover versions. There was "Red Red Wine" (which gave me a headache whenever I accidentally caught it on the radio), "I Got You Babe" with Chrissie Hynde from The Pretenders (doing a great job of pretending she thought they were any good) and "(I Can't Help) Falling In Love With You" (which I couldn't help fucking hating).

Their best known album was *Labour of Love*, which was a collection of covers. It sold so well they later released *Labour of Love II* and *Labour of Love III*. Those albums might well have been a Labour of Love for the band, but for the poor misguided listener, they were more like vinyl afterbirth – a waste of time, messy and shoved out by twats.

Ultravox

One of the most amusing moments in 1980s pop history was when Ultravox unleashed their 'epic' single "Vienna" in 1981, and Joe Dolce's record "Shaddap You Face" kept it off the number one spot. If the British public preferred a dire novelty record featuring pidgin English and an awful Italian accent, it doesn't say much about what they thought of Ultravox's magnum opus. Obviously, it meant nothing to them. Like it meant nothing to me. Ah, Vienna…

Vanilla Ice

Pop Star popular around 1990

You can understand why Robert Van Winkle chose not to use his real name when embarking upon a career in rap. A white rapper was a laughable enough prospect back at the beginning of the 1990s, but there was no chance at all of being taken seriously with a name that made him sound like a Dutch investment banker. So Robert swapped his amusing original moniker for another equally entertaining one – Vanilla Ice. It was a clever choice. He was white, so Vanilla. He thought he was cool, so Ice. And every time we heard him "rocking the mic like a vandal" we creamed ourselves with laughter. Perfect. A Mr Whippy hairdo completed the image.

Robert's main problem wasn't his name, however, or his laughable sense of style, but simply the fact that no one believed he was this rough and tough punk

Ice invents a new game: Rock, paper, or dickhead with scissors.

from the street that he made himself out to be. The only caps he popped were the ones in his cowboy gun when he was playing wigwams at the next-door neighbours. Even New Kids on the Block would have turned Ice down for being too middle class and lame. If indeed he had any street cred at all, it was seriously overdrawn.

Then there was the music. Again, Rob got into trouble here as he insisted on borrowing other people's tunes. "Ice Ice Baby", his major hit, used elements from "Under Pressure", the Queen and Bowie collaboration, but the silly billy forgot to ask for permission. Another single covered "Play That Funky Music" but it slipped his mind to bother acknowledging the original songwriter, which led to legal problems. His debut album was even blander than vanilla. Sales dried up after his 1990 number one single, and fortunately for us, the Iceman wenteth.

Vesta Curries

The national dish these days is curry. Freshly prepared in one of the UK's many curry houses, or purchased ready to cook from supermarkets, there's a wide selection of spicy variations to choose from. Chicken tikka masala for the connoisseur who likes his food to be a hue that nature never intended, and vindaloo, usually eaten by a man who's half asbestos, half lager, and half tattoos (and who can't add up very well). But in the 1960s and 1970s, when fish and chips was still Britain's favourite meal, having a curry was the height of culinary daring. It showed you had a sophisticated and worldly palette. Skegness might be as far east as your body had travelled, but your tongue had been to Bombay (and your arse to hell and back).

However, it wasn't particularly easy to get hold of a curry back then, simply because there weren't that many restaurants around. In fact the only real way to sate your urge for something spicy was to rush down to Kwik Save and pick up a Vesta. This was a DIY curry which was available in a choice of flavours, none of which were particularly hot or indeed curry-like. The box contained sachets of coloured powder which you prepared by tipping into a pot of boiling hot water and stirring. The end result was a shiny brown stew that both looked and tasted like shit. And which made your kitchen stink like a Calcutta cesspit.

Mind you, that was partially the idea. Eating the food was optional. Preparing it was the important thing. You wanted your neighbours to know you were having a truly exotic meal – not fish fingers and chips like them – and a good Vesta could stench out the house for days on end.

But your sophistication didn't need to be contained within the four walls of your home. Oh no. You could impress the girl of your dreams by going round to her house and casually asking to use the toilet. The resulting smell left people in no doubt just how urbane you were. You could see the respect in their bulging eyes as they darted in, cheeks puffed out, to open a window.

The mark of how classy a family was lay in whether they celebrated your cultural exchange programme, or tried to overpower it with a splash of Brut. Back in the days of Vesta there was no accounting for taste.

Village People

Pop Group popular around 1978–80

There's only one gay in the village, according to *Little Britain*. There were a few more than that in the Village People, which came as no surprise to anyone given their appearance. The biker in leathers, the construction worker, Indian chief, cowboy, military officer and policeman – along with their camp disco dance routines, they looked more queen than Freddy Mercury.

While the homosexual stereotypes of the moustachioed leather-clad biker and big burly builder were pretty obvious selections, the group missed out on some blatant opportunities. Where was the politician? Or the vicar? Or the judge complete with luminous pink wig? These were far better ideas than some of the weaker costumes they had in the line-up. The military bloke for example – what was that all about? What were they trying to suggest? That people in the army were gay? A clearly absurd notion. Everybody knows full well that it's the navy you join

Their early career as eco-warriors wasn't very successful, as the trees they were trying to protect all died of shame.

if it's men's bottoms you admire. Why else do you think they call them Rear Admirals? And indeed one of the band's biggest hits was "In The Navy", which the US Navy allegedly commissioned to use in their recruitment adverts, until they realized the sort of seaman the Village People were really trying to procure on a nightly basis.

However, the group's most famous tune – and moreover dance – was "YMCA". It was a big success mainly because everyone could do the chorus moves, spelling out the letters Y-M-C-A with their arms. Everyone apart from dyslexics, that is, who got thoroughly pissed off with the whole thing, and possibly confused onlookers into thinking the song was also part of an ad campaign for the American department store chain Macy's.

Come the 1980s, the Village People realized they had to move with the times or perish, so they reinvented themselves as a new wave band. And quickly perished. Probably because they weren't quite camp enough for the new romantic scene.

Vinyl Records — Music Format popular around 1950–90

Although vinyl records are still pressed in small numbers, it's pretty much a defunct music format now. Don't let a music snob – sorry, an "audiophile" (sounds like someone who likes their stereo just a little bit too much to me) – hear you say that, though. Because then you'll undoubtedly be in for a very tedious lecture about how today's CDs are digital and lifeless, whereas the vinyl of yesteryear had an extra sonic dimension which was warm, vibrant and alive.

Exactly how a sound can be warm I'm not sure, but I think what they mean is that it sounds a lot like someone's urinating on the record as it's played. I certainly remember a lot of hissing and spattering noises coming out of the speakers when I used to listen to my vinyl collection. The reason for this, of course, is that records are delicate things; they generally suffer more scratches than a cat with scabies, and are prone to warping more frequently than the Starship Enterprise.

CDs can skip as well, but the difference there is you can simply wipe a CD down with a soft cloth and it'll be fine again. Restoring vinyl is like attempting to glue the Mona Lisa back together after a shredding accident. Vinyl, incidentally, is short for polyvinyl chloride, or, as it's better known, PVC. Yep, records are made from the same stuff as gimp suits – mention you're into "vinyl" in the wrong areas of London and you could end up as warped as your 33s album collection.

The final and most compelling argument against vinyl must surely be that copies of Terry Wogan's "Floral Dance" still exist on the format. They don't on CD. If that doesn't persuade you that the warm sound of records should really be the crackling of them melting on giant "Fahrenheit 451"-style bonfires, then nothing will.

Wash & Go — Hair Product popular around 1989–95

"Take two bottles into the shower? Not me, I just Wash & Go!" Ooohh, well aren't you fucking clever? The idea that you could save time and effort when in the shower by using a combination shampoo and conditioner took the UK by storm back in 1989. Stupid really, when you think about it. We wouldn't have jumped up and down in excitement if someone had announced they'd managed to blend a vindaloo with eight pints of lager, would we? ("I just eat… and throw!")

Wash & Go was aimed exclusively at women. It's obvious because the phrase "wash and go" has slightly different connotations for a man. To us that simply means the usual morning routine of a quick lather up and a piss in the shower.

So did Wash & Go save a generation of women all that time in the bathroom? Of course not. It simply gave them a little longer to shave their legs and armpits, to use their special moisturising shower crème and exfoliate their faces with small pieces of crushed apricot kernels. Apparently it took scientists three years to come up with Wash & Go. Three years! Saving you having to take two bottles into the shower? Not exactly on a par with cloning sheep is it? Presumably they spent most of that time waiting for the lab beagle's hair to grow long enough to test the stuff.

Weebles
Toy popular around 1971–85

The Weebles were a race of small fat plastic folk shaped like eggs. They had a heavy (quite possibly lead) weight in their bottoms which, along with their oval shape, meant that no matter how hard you pushed them around, they wouldn't topple over. Or, as the advertising jingle phrased it: "Weebles wobble but they don't fall down." A bit like drunk people, although mercifully Weebles didn't insist on calling you their best mate every seven seconds.

What the ad people hadn't taken into account was the naturally curious nature of their target market. Kids across the land wanted (or rather *needed*) to know if this phenomenon was something unique to Weebles, or if all fat people had an innate ability to stay upright in a variety of testing situations. This inquisitiveness led to porky pupils across the land being repeatedly charged into, shoved hard from behind in surprise playground attacks or pushed off the top of stairwells. These days that kind of action might be frowned on and called bullying, but back then it was serious scientific study.

Fatty Patterson fell down when you rammed him into the school lockers, but would he topple over when two of you struck him at different angles by the school gates? And what about if you unexpectedly backed into him hard during assembly? The results of this impromptu countrywide experiment were universally consistent: Weebles wobble, but they don't fall down. Fat kids wobble and they fall down surprisingly easily.

Wet Wet Wet

Shit Shit Shit.

Wham!

George Michael sang in a slightly camp voice. He wore leathers, had impossibly immaculate coiffured hair, deeply sun-tanned skin, and he liked to show off his oiled torso from time to time. But no matter how loudly George screamed his homosexuality back in the 1980s, nobody heard him. NO ONE. It was the decade in which the public's gaydar was seriously broken.

When we look back at those old Wham videos now, it's obvious. He couldn't have come across any gayer if he'd been mincing across the stage in an arse-less fairy costume. Yeah, in some of the shoots they had him canoodling with women, but even then you can clearly see in his eyes that he's a plumber trying to rewire a house. Of course, whether he was gay or not made no difference to Wham's musical prowess. They were still abysmal. Ever disposable, their pop ran the entire gamut of inanity, from the superficiality of "Young Guns (Go For It)" through to the utter nonsense of "Wake Me Up Before You Go-Go". Possibly the most

Tweedledum and Tweedledumber.

stupidly named song ever:

"The title's got to fit with the rest of the chorus lines – what rhymes with 'solo' Andy?"

"Go?"

"Yeah, but that's a bit short and doesn't scan."

"Hmm… Go-Go?"

"Genius! We'll call it that. And what about the album?"

"Wham-Wham?"

George might have penned the inspirational lyrics, and arranged the music, and sung the vocals, but he was only half of Wham. The other half(wit) was Andrew Ridgeley, who, erm, well, hung around in the background pretending he could play the guitar. And made the tea.

The band's T-shirts urged us to "Choose Life", but I preferred to choose deaf. A decision which made me deliriously happy when it came to the sound of Wham.

White Dog Turds — Excrement popular around 1960–85

Here's absolute proof that people will get nostalgic over any old shit. In this case, old white dog shit. "Oh, whatever happened to white dog poo?" they'll sometimes ask, all misty-eyed over a pint at the local, as if they missed it like a long-lost friend…

Who cares what colour dog crap is? Even if it was rainbow coloured and there was a small pot of gold at the end of it, you still wouldn't want to stand in one of the bastards.

If you really must have an answer to the long-standing "what happened to it" cliché, any good dog shit historian will tell you that the white stuff is simply poop that has been bleached by the sun (shit hot, if you will). It disappeared because school bullies insisted on continually rolling little kids in dog turds, so the council started cleaning them up more thoroughly, meaning it wasn't left to bake for long enough. If you don't believe me, try it yourself – crap on a shovel and leave it out on the patio in the sun for a few weeks, then record your findings for posterity. Or posteriority perhaps.

So forget your urban myths and conspiracy theories. It was nothing to do with the old worming tablets vets used to give mutts, or the fact that bones were more prevalent in yesteryear's canine diet, so there was more calcium in the turds. Neither was it anything to do with aliens. Everyone knows their shit's bright purple.

White Socks — Clothes popular around 1980–84

The 1980s was responsible for a whole load of odd fashion innovations. One of which, for reasons that I don't think will ever be successfully explained, was the sudden rise in popularity of white socks. It didn't matter what colour trousers you wore – black school slacks, blue jeans, burgundy stapress – you could only wear one colour of sock, and that was white. Having your trousers too short so they swung around your ankles helped to show off this cutting-edge fashion statement.

Girls weren't too impressed with boring old white socks and upped the ante by choosing to wear fluorescent ones instead. These came in a range of disgusting colours (pink, green, orange and yellow) which were designed never to be seen together and yet, predictably, ended up being combined.

Boys could, and did, sometimes wear the pink variation, but that was usually down to mum accidentally washing their white socks with a red bra.

Why Don't You? — TV Programme popular around 1975–85

Why Don't You was an arts and crafts style show for kids which was shown by the BBC during the school holidays. It suggested things for bored pre-teens to do instead of watching television, and it was actually presented by children from different cities dotted about the UK. One week it would be the "Liverpool gang", then the turn of the "Bristol gang" and so on.

Which only serves to illustrate what an entirely more innocent era this was. A gang of Bristol nippers these days wouldn't be showing other tykes how to make a magic trick from four toilet roll tubes and a piece of sandpaper, oh no. They'd probably be demonstrating how to cut your coke with the correct amount of baking soda. And the Liverpool gang might do a section on how to break into a Ford Focus with a coat-hanger in under a minute.

Mind you, that would be more interesting than the crap jokes, misguided cookery lessons and *Blue Peter* style drivel the youthful hosts did churn out. It was quite ironic that the punch-line of the show's theme tune was "Why don't you just switch off your television set and go and do something less boring instead?" Just how apt was that? When you heard it, if you switched straight off as instructed, you'd definitely be far less bored for the following half an hour, even if you spent it helping auntie sort her button collection into different colours.

The Word — TV Programme popular around 1990–95

An edgy youth-driven Channel 4 show, *The Word* encompassed live music, chat and all sorts of bizarre features. Terry Christian for one. He was the main presenter, which meant the programme was about as well presented as your average octogenarian tramp. When Terry wasn't spewing verbal diarrhoea out onto your living room carpet in his grating Mancunian tones, he was floundering around completely lost, staring gormlessly into the camera while he paused in confusion before stumbling and stuttering his way through another fluffed link.

The Word was, quite simply, bloody awful bloody chaos. Sure, some entertaining and shocking things happened, as you would expect on a live late-night show targeted at those returning home from the pub. Like when the lead singer of L7 flashed her triangle (and not the musical variety) at the close of their performance. The worst stuff was generally reserved for "The Hopefuls" though, a section of the programme in which people who would do anything to get on TV did, well, anything to get on TV. This led to one particularly horrendous snippet of televisual history in which a young guy French kissed an old granny. On the plus side, at least Terry Christian wasn't on camera for those thirty seconds.

Fortunately, Terry wasn't the only presenter on *The Word*. There was also Mark "I have a greasy facsimile of Ayer's Rock perched atop my head" Lamarr, Katie "I've shaved half my eyebrow off and it's the most interesting thing about me" Puckrik, and Amanda "What camera am I on, what does that cue card say, who am I talking to, why am I talking to them and why do I even exist?" De Cadenet. She was, to all intents and purposes, the female equivalent of Christian, but with a marginally less annoying accent. In later shows the producers brought in new faces, such as Dani Behr, who replaced Amanda as the tottering totty, but she could Behr-ly present either and *The Word* still managed to go downhill (which was quite an achievement – about its only one).

If a Bible was written to cover the 1990s – the newer testament, perhaps – it could open like this: "In the beginning was *The Word*, and *The Word* was shit. And shit was *The Word*." What came next wouldn't really matter, as everyone would be hastily thumbing forward to find the bit where Christian gets eaten by the lions.

Worzel Gummidge — TV Programme popular around 1979–81

Worzel was the star of his own kids' TV series. He was a living scarecrow, like the one out of *The Wizard of Oz*. Of course, Dorothy's mate didn't have a brain, whereas Worzel had approximately 26. You see, he had an expansive inventory of spare heads which he could swap at will, one for each and every occasion. If two heads were better than one, by rights Worzel should have been bloody ace! But he wasn't. Worzel was a dick. His bonce collection was total rubbish. He

Was there anything in Worzel's pants? Only the Crowman knew.

could have ordered some really cool heads to be made by his creator, the Crowman, like a Superman head with laser eyes. Or an *Exorcist* head which span round and projectile vomited. That would've seen more than the crows off. Or a sex head with a two foot long tongue (he'd have pulled love interest Aunt Sally with that on). He could've had some fun.

But no. Worzel had a singing head, which could, well, sing. And a fishing head, with which he could go fishing (I think this one doubled as his sleeping head). And a boring bastard head. Wait a minute, that was simply his default model. Perhaps the best episode of *Worzel Gummidge* – when I say best, naturally I mean least painfully tedious – was the one where he was put on trial and faced the death penalty. The prospect of an ex-Gummidge was a very appealing one. Predictably, he got let off, which was probably just as well as had he been executed the episode could have run on infinitely. "Off with his head! And his other head… and his other…"

Wrestling

These days, wrestling is big business, and all about perma-tanned musclemen dressing up in lycra and playing at superheroes by dancing with each other. Back in the 1970s, it was an amateurish activity largely staged in smoky town halls which gained a surprising following thanks to its regular Saturday afternoon slot on *World of Sport*.

Strange as it might seem now, back then wrestling was considered a proper sport. It was just like boxing, except that hitting your opponent was replaced with bouncing off ropes, belly flops and rolling around on the floor like a two-year-old throwing a tantrum. And with fat bastards in place of highly trained athletes.

The top wrestlers still had nicknames, but instead of The Rock, The Undertaker, Hulk Hogan and Sgt. Slaughter we had the rather less impressive sounding Big Daddy, Giant Haystacks and Kendo Nagasaki, who for no discernible reason always went into the ring wearing a gimp mask.

Shirley's moves might not have been dazzling, but his top hat was.

Our wrestlers didn't have entourages, theme tunes or flying leaps off the top rope either. Although to be fair, Giant Haystacks was 6'11" tall and weighed 49 stone, which meant he got out of breath just climbing into the ring. If he'd tried anything vaguely acrobatic it would probably have ended with the Earth being ripped from its axis and sent hurtling into deep space.

If a wrestler attempted to do anything against the rules they were likely to get a warning for bad behaviour. If they did it again, they got disqualified. This didn't happen all that often though because, as with wrestling today, everything was carefully choreographed beforehand. We just didn't know it at the time. The idea that it might not be a genuine tussle between two exceptionally tubby sportsmen never crossed our minds.

It was only when we discovered that Big Daddy's real name was Shirley Crabtree that we began to have doubts. In 1985 wrestling disappeared from Saturday afternoon schedules, replaced by actual sport. This was a shame for many, but not me, as it meant I no longer had to wrestle with my dad. It was hard work fighting desperately to get to the TV so I could change channels and put something decent on.

X-Ray Specs

Advertised in American comics, X-Ray Specs appeared to be a technological marvel. Despite only costing a few dollars, they enabled you to see the bones in your hand, the lead in a pencil, the yolk of an egg… and other "blushingly funny" amazing things too. Which adolescent boys the world over took to mean just one thing. They could be used to see through girls' clothing.

It was, sadly, all tosh. The glasses were cheap plastic things with cardboard lenses. Each lens had a small hole in it, and across this hole was a white feather. When you looked through the vanes of the feather you saw two offset images – a darker one inside, and a lighter one outside. So, for example, when you looked at your hand through the specs, you saw what appeared to be bones. When you looked at Cathy Bates in the school playground you saw through the claims in the ad and realized you'd wasted a week's pocket money to look like a gullible pervert.

Yahtzee

Milton Bradley's Yahtzee was at the height of its popularity in the early 1980s, when the adverts showed an aspirational group of middle class folk crowded around the game. The dice would be rolled and everyone would excitedly yell "Yahtzee" before taking a sip of their gin and tonics and nodding agreeably at each other.

Yahtzee was basically a posh person's version of draw poker, played with five dice instead of cards which were rolled into the game's green plastic box. You had two chances to re-roll any dice you didn't like before having to record the score of your hand, which just like poker could be three of a kind, a full house or the top scoring Yahtzee (five of a kind – which isn't in poker, not unless you're a really bad cheat). If you got that, you could yell "Yahtzee" just like on the ads, and then all your friends could sip from their gin and tonics and laugh at you for being such a twat.

The fun bit of poker, the betting, was replaced with working out where to place your dice rolls on the score-sheet to obtain the most points. In other words, the high stakes bluffing and nail biting tension were ousted in favour of some maths. Which was a stroke of genius. Well, maybe not, but someone definitely pulled a stroke somewhere with Yahtzee, simply by managing to sell dice in a box for fifteen quid. There was only ever going to be one winner of that particular game – the Milton Bradley directors' wallets, which were no doubt royally flush.

Yuppie

The word yuppie was used in the 1980s to signify a Young Upwardly Mobile Professional. Or, to put it another way, a high earning prat with slicked-back hair and red braces. If you were a yuppie there were certain things you had to do. Such as dress to impress in a power suit (sadly not something that gave you super powers), carry a filofax everywhere, even to the toilet – it could come in handy if there was no toilet paper there – drink in a wine bar rather than a pub, and drive either a BMW or a Porsche.

Yuppies also had to work in the city and dabble in the market. It didn't really matter if the city was Norwich, they worked in telesales, and the market primarily sold fish, so long as they could truthfully make that claim. In 1987 the film *Wall Street* showed the rest of us just what an exciting yuppie life we were missing out on and told us "greed was good." However, shortly afterwards the market crashed and the yuppies suddenly found themselves in trouble. As the joke went, unlike pigeons, these once high flying rats could no longer make a deposit on a Porsche. Something all non-yuppies agreed was good.

ZX81

Sir Clive Sinclair's second home computer (following the ZX80) was a massive success, selling hundreds of thousands across the UK. God knows why. It didn't have anything approximating a real keyboard – you had to type on a membrane-meets-bubblewrap hybrid – and its blocky black and white graphics were pathetic. It was nicknamed the "doorstop" by some, because it was a solid lump of black plastic which was next to useless in computing terms, only having 1k of base memory, which was a laughable amount even back then.

You could upgrade the memory to a whopping 16k with an add-on module, but unfortunately it wasn't the most stable of extras. Halfway through typing in a long program listing, someone flushing a toilet three streets away would be enough to break the fragile link and cause the whole computer to reset itself. Ram pack wobble (to use its technical name) was a serious problem. Enterprising kids would try to shore up the connection with copious amounts of Blu-tac and brown parcel tape but nailing it in place would have been a better idea. The nail might have knackered the entire computer, but that was for the best anyway, as the ZX81 could then be put to some real use – propping open the study door.